BUSTER
The Silver Tip Grizzly

BUSTER
The Silver Tip Grizzly

Franklin Thomas Briles
Dyerville, California
-1902-

To order additional copies of this book, contact:
Xlibris Corporation
1-888-795-4274
www.Xlibris.com
Orders@Xlibris.com
58434

Newly weds Franklin Thomas and Mayme Briles fishing on
the Eel River circa 1915

FOREWORD

Gone is the era when a rugged 17 year-old first-time bear hunter could take off into the hills, saying "I'll be back."

This is a tale of raw spirit and adventure as a young bear hunter becomes a bear's best friend and trainer.

Read the adventures of Buster and Franklin as they relocate from California to Oklahoma and take to the stage.

Although this story took place in 1902, it wasn't until 1926 that Buster's story was put down on paper.

"We watched and listened while my father dictated the story and my mother typed and typed and retyped trying to get it right. It seemed to take forever," son Franklin says.

The original manuscript, kept in a "Scholastic" two-ring binder until 2009, is now protected and reproduced for our family and others to enjoy.

Dyerville, California

BUSTER
THE SILVER TIP GRIZZLY

Before I start to tell my story of my pet, which was a trained silver tip grizzly bear, I want to give you an idea as to the different species of bears. Science has found that there are over twenty species, there being five different kinds of grizzlys, some of which especially in California have become extinct in the past twenty five years. These grizzlys vary in size, some obtaining the weight of over a thousand pounds. The color varying from a buff to a very dark brown, but when coming out in the spring after hibernation, the hairs are tipped with silver, thus giving them the name of silver tip grizzly.

From the earliest history in America, the grizzly has been known as the most dangerous of big game. To the Indian, it was considered a very high honor to obtain a necklace of grizzly claws. But the white man with his high powered guns have changed conditions so that the grizzly is now much more shy than before, for at the slightest noise he will run away at a surprisingly rapid speed. The grizzly is very dangerous and if cornered will put up a fight and many hunters have been killed by them, especially if a bear is wounded. The grizzly is considered the most intelligent of all the species and to my knowledge is more intelligent than any other animal. Their sense of hearing is very keen and their scent is as keen as the deer, being able to scent their enemy at a great distance. Their eyes are very small but have the keenest of sight. They have forty two teeth, the same as the dog and are carnivorous, eating besides animal flesh, fish, birds, eggs, leaves, fruit and honey, even grubs and reptiles, especially fond of anything sweet. As to cleanliness, they are not particular. The claws of the grizzlys are especially different from other bears as they are long and slender and are slightly curved. They attain the length of more than three inches and the tracks of the grizzly in damp sand, measure sometimes over twelve inches.

The Alaskan Brown Bear is somewhat larger than the grizzly, sometimes been known to weigh over fifteen hundred pounds, and is the largest living carnivorous land animal, standing more than four feet high at the shoulder and attains the length of nine and one half feet. This specie was discovered on the Kodiak Island in about 1895. During the large salmon run, these bears live chiefly on fish, bur during the summer they eat grass and many other plans, also spend much time in hunting mice and ground squirrel.

The Black Bear or Cinnamon Bear as it is more commonly known, is generally found all over the United States, especially in the wooded areas. The color of these bears is black with a small portion of brown over the nose, their weight being much less than the grizzly, which is about three hundred pounds to five hundred pounds. They are considered harmless and in most areas are protected. They are commonly seen in the National Parks and are quite tame. Their habits of eating are very similar to other bears, being chiefly berries, acorns, honey and fruits of all kinds. They also hibernate as do the other bears.

The Glacier Bear is another specie, closely related to the Black Bear, although it is of a light bluish gray to a dark gray. It lives in the northwestern part of Alaska, in the glacier region and his habits are very similar to other bears but very few have been killed or captured.

Now the Polar Bear is very different from all other bears as it is an all white bear, having a much longer neck and slender hand, also has fur which covers the soles of his feet. The Polar Bear lives most all of its' life on the ice but when hungry and food is scarce, it hunts on the barren islands of the Arctic zone. Its' food consists of fish, seals, walrus and what scanty vegetation can be found on the islands. These bears will not attack man unless extremely hungry or cornered. They are very powerful swimmers. Unlike other bears, it is only the female bear who hibernates and during this time the cubs are born and she stays with them until they are nearly half grown. All cubs are born in the winter months, are naked and very small, most of them weighing less than a pound and also have their eyes closed which do not open for almost a month. It takes about another month before the cubs are able to follow the mother and she takes care of them practically all summer and it has been known that they hibernate the following winter with the mother.

The first scene of my story is located in Humbolt County, in the northern part of California and happened over thirty years ago, at that time my mother operated a hotel in the small town of Dyerville which is located on the Eel River where the North Fork and South Fork of the Eel River join. This was at that time a stage depot, where the passengers usually stayed overnight to rest and where the horses were changed for the stages.

At this time, the stage line was owned and operated by my brother-in-law A.P. Cross, and which runs between Ukiah and Eureka California, a distance of about two hundred miles.

Now if any of you readers were to make this trip on one of these stages or carts, you would think that it was about five hundred miles. At that time during the winter months when the rains were so great and so many slides and mud, carts were used most of the time and it took from four to six head of horses to pull them. The carts had two wheels which were very large and not over three passengers were allowed to ride, as the mail was the main thing to get to its' destination. When placed in the cart you were strapped in and then covered with mail pouches, with just your head sticking out and straps and ropes were placed over the mail pouches for the stage company took no chances of loosing any of the mail or passengers on the way. The average speed was about seven or eight miles per hour. It was so much fun to ride on these carts that it made a well man sick and a sick man well and you were certainly glad when you reached your journeys end.

In the fall of 1902, I made a trip to Dyerville to visit my mother for the winter. At this time this country was noted for its fine fishing and hunting, there being quite a quantity of mountain lions, bear and an abundance of deer. The Eel River was noted for the spawning grounds of the salmon. I have seen a school of salmon so large that when trying to get over the ripples, they would be so think that they would shove each other out on the sand bars. It looked like it would be very simple to pick one up with his hands but it was not as easy as it looked. It took a spear to get one as these fish vary in weight, fifteen to seventy five pounds and unless you were a regular he-man, it would be out of the question to land one with the bare hands.

Early one morning I started out with my spear for one of the ripples, to bring in a couple of salmon for the hotel and as I was crossing a sand bar, I noticed the tracks of a large bear and two small cub tracks. I examined the tracks very carefully and knowing that they were not over an hour or so old, forgetting all about the salmon, I returned to the hotel to make preparations to go after the bear.

There was a young man working at the hotel by the name of Pat and I asked him if he would like to go with me on this bear chase. He said that he had never trailed or hunted bear but would sure take a chance and go along. I told him that the tracks were as large as elephant tracks and I was sure that they were grizzly tracks. At that time there was quite a large bounty on grizzly bears, so it meant a chance to pick up some money as well as the sport of it.

I told Pat, lets get busy and get things together as that bear and cubs can be ten miles away in a few hours. First I will go down and see Mr. Carland and find out if he will let us have his bear dogs as it would be out of the question to go without dogs.

Mr. Carland consented to let me have his three dogs and explained to me that these dogs would mind me as he had let them go on lion and bear hunts with friends. He kept them chained most of the time, the first one he unchained was a very small dog, no doubt but that he was half cur and half rat terrier, his name being Ring. The next dog he unchained was another small dog, named Mickie, being a mixture of hound and cur and the third dog was named Buster, this dog being mostly hound and a wee bit of shepherd and he was real dog.

Taking the three dogs with me, I then went back to the hotel to get the guns, ammunition, one blanket for each of us, some bacon, coffee, bread, eagle brand milk, etc. We told everyone good-bye and started out. There were several old stage drivers sitting around and made remarks such as "There goes two great bear hunters and they will be back before the sun goes down and will glad to get back", but never-the-less they did not know the half of it.

We arrived at the river and found the tracks and kept Buster, the largest dog on a rope, as he had a very keen scent, and the main thing for us was for us to follow the dog. The two small dogs never got over five hundred feet away from us at any time. We were on the South fork of the Eel River and tacked the old mother bear and two cubs up this stream for about three miles. She was very foxy, at times where the water was shallow enough so that both she and the cubs could wade, they would stay in the water for a distance of several hundred feet at a time. She did this so that a dog could not get the scent of her tracks, also so that a hunter would not be able to trail her. We came to a small stream leading off to the north east, up which the bear and two cubs went.

Up to this time we had very easy traveling, but just the same we sat down to take a rest and were just on the outer edge of the Redwood Flats. Pat suggested that we take a smoke but I warned him that the mother bear would scent this tobacco smoke for a great distance but noticed that the wind was in the opposite direction of the bear tracks, so decided that it would be alright. As Pat sat there with a stick in his hand poking in the dirt, he said "Do you know anything about bear hunting?" "Well, I haven't had very much experience at bear hunting but have hunted a lot of deer in this vicinity." "The main thing is, I want to be sure that you know this country and that we going to get home without getting lost."

"Now don't you worry about that, just get your gun and lets beat it. Here you take this rope and let Buster drag you along for a while but be mighty careful and do not let him get away from you, for if you do, it will be all off. He will catch up with the bears in a little while as you know the mother bear cannot travel very fast for the cubs must be quite small. Just take a look at these cub tracks, I do not believe these cubs are over four months old. Of course if she did not have the cubs, I do not think we would stand a chance of catching up with her. I have been told by several old hunters that these bear can make thirty or forty miles per day in the roughest country and I think it would be mighty hard for either you or I to go that far in one day and right now this old Ingersol tells me it is about time to eat."

"Well I have been waiting a long time for you to say that and here is something I am going to surprise you with. When I was in the kitchen of the hotel, just before we left and you were getting some of the chuck to take along with us, I saw this can of corn beef and also your mother gave me these biscuits and doughnuts."

"We will eat the corn beef but lets keep the doughnuts as a reserve. It is about one o'clock now and we must have come about six miles and if the bear keeps following this stream, we will get into the roughest country in Humbolt County. It surely is a hard thing to keep those small dogs back but if this hound should ever get loose, they would all catch up with the bear and we might as well turn around and go home."

"We have now been climbing for the past two or three hours and no doubt but that we are about two thousand feet altitude and you know these bears travel for the high country and the very roughest they can find. Now Pat, I think we are rushing a little too fast, we will have to take a bit more time or we are going to find ourselves pretty tired." "I do not think we are rushing too fast, it is Buster who is doing all the rushing."

"Stop Pat and look right ahead of you, up on the third limb of that tree and you will see two gray squirrels. Do you see them?" "Yes, I see them." "Well here is a good place to try out your marksmanship."

So Pat took his rifle and brought down one of the squirrels but it was too badly shot for us to eat but it would be a good feed for the dogs and I told him we should at least have two or three more.

While I was skinning the squirrel, Pat discovered what is known as a pickle snail or at least that is what an old man in Oregon told me they were called. "Now if you want to see something funny or strange, just light a match and hold it close to the snail and it will begin to melt just as though it were a chunk of ice." "Do you think that it will die?" Pat asked. But the funniest thing was, that when Pat took the match way, say in eight or ten minutes, the snail began to contract and become a solid mass again.

Pat said, "Well, I never saw anything like that in my life and I don't think many other people have seen anything like it either, but just the same it is true." Pat suggested taking the snail along with us but I told him we haven't yet go to that stage, where we would have to eat snails.

"We must get going as we have fooled enough time away. Did you ever see a more beautiful stream than this one, the water is just as clear as a crystal and ferns and undergrowth so beautiful and green and enormous size. You talk about trout, just look at them."

It was beginning to look as though we would have to find a place to spend the night as in another forty minutes it would be dark and when it gets dark in these forests, it is dark. We had only gone another few hundred feet when I noticed an old tree which had fallen many years ago and the inside had been burned out. I could see back in it for some twelve or fifteen feet and I said, "I think this is where we will stay for the night. You rustle up some wood and build a fire and I will cut some of these ferns and put them in the tree for our bed."

We had bacon and biscuits for our supper and then sat around the campfire talking until both of us became pretty sleepy. "What do you say, lets turn in. We will take the dogs in with us and I will tie the rope which is fastened to Buster through the button hole of my coat, as we will sleep with all of our clothes on but will pull our boots off so our feet will get a rest."

After we had been in bed for a short time, Pat said, "I don't think this bear hunting is what it is cracked up to be and my mother didn't raise me to be a bear hunter." "Old boy, you better get to sleep for we are going to get out of here at day break." Pat said, "I sure wish that the break of day was here right now for I do not think I am going to sleep any."

We finally got to sleep and got a real good rest and in the morning as we crawled out of the old charred tree trunk, I took just one look at Pat and began to laugh, and he asked me, "What are you laughing at", and by that time he took one look at me and he also began to laugh and said, "Well you look as though you were ready to join the Minstrel Show." During the night we had gotten the black from the charred tree trunk on our hands and then rubbed our face. Now we surely had some time getting this off of our face as we had no soap with us and almost had to scour our faces with sand to get clean.

"Well, lets make the coffee and flapjacks and get on our way for we have a big day ahead of us." So as soon as our breakfast was over, we started out.

"Now Pat, it sure looks as though this bear has headed for the North Fork of the Eel, which runs a way up in the Blue Rock district and I have been told that the altitude runs as high as ten thousand feet and when one gets up that high and carrying these blankets, heavy rifles and food, also with these heavy boots, which have a half pound of hob nails in them, it won't be long until we will be reaching for our breath. No doubt but that we will know something in the next few hours and I made up my mind when we left Dyerville, I was going to get these bears and I don't intend to let those fellows give us the horselaugh when we get back." Pat spoke up, "I am sure glad that you feel that way about it, but I know one thing for sure, I would feel a lot better if I had stayed back there at the hotel."

"You are not getting cold feet are you?" Of course this being our first night out, it did seem a bit tough but with such good dogs and our rifles there was practically no danger, so I said "Cheer up and get a smile on your face, things will look better later on."

We were surely in some very rough country and had not gone very far, when we had the surprise of our life. We were still following the stream, when all at once we heard the two small dogs, Ring and Mickie barking as loud as they could. It was all that we could do to hold Buster back and I said, "Pat, they surely have her treed or cornered. I will tie Buster to this tree and put our packs right here as they are not over four or five hundred feet ahead of us." We went about two hundred feet but as yet had not located them, so I suggested that we leave the stream and work up above them and we could then look down on both the dogs and the bears and gets a much better shot. We then worked down closer to the stream and could see the two dogs barking and looking up into the old tree which had fallen half way across the stream but we could see nothing. I whispered to Pat, "I bet those dogs have a coon or possum up that tree." So when we had worked our way down to within about seventy feet of the tree, we had a great surprise, for there was a large panther or in other words a mountain lion. These lions are very dangerous and if once crippled or hurt in any way, they will attack and nine times out of ten, it is death. She was stretched out on one of the large limbs of the tree and when the dogs would bark, she would growl and show her teeth. I figured that we were in close range and could shoot as it was not over seventy five or one hundred feet but the location we were in made it very difficult to get a good shot at her head or heart, as we were up too high and looking down on her, so I began to work my way to the north so as to get a side shot.

We did not bring Buster with us as we wanted him to guard our food and we could hear him making a terrible fuss. I began to get worried that the panther would make a spring onto the two dogs, but all at once she located us and made a half turn and looked right at us and gave a snarl. I said to Pat, "What do you think of that smile, I think she means business and real quick." I told Pat to take the first shot but to be sure to shoot to kill. He said, "No, I would rather that you do the shooting."

"Well here goes." I took dead aim right at her head as her face was toward me. I hit my mark and she fell right down into the water. We both made a wild scramble and in a few seconds we were where she had fallen into the water. The stream was not very large but quite swift and I waded out into the water and as she came by me I made a grab for her and by the time Pat and I both got hold of her, we dragged her onto the bank. She must have weighed at least two hundred pounds and no doubt she was at least eight feet long form nose to tip of tail.

Pat asked, "What are you going to do with her, now that you have killed her?" I answered, "I am going to skin her and take the hide home with me."

All at once I noticed that her body began to move and I said to Pat, "I don't believe she is dead, but I could not figure out why as half of her head was shot off." It then came to me quickly, that she was carrying her young and that they were still alive.

"Now Pat, there is going to be what they call a Caesarian operation. You go get Buster and the packs as I need the ropes off the packs to hang this panther up on a limb." "I am not going any place unless you go with me, the mate to that panther might be here some place."

I did not like to leave the panther there as I was afraid the dogs would attack her and chew on her, but never-the-less, I went with Pat and brought the two packs and Buster. We then managed to get her hung up in the tree and I started the surgical work. I tried to be very careful as I knew that a fatal move with this sharp hunting knife would mean death to the tiny kittens. This was very exciting to both of us and we were rather nervous but just the same we got a laugh or two. I managed to get the four kittens from the mother without injuring them in any way. I had a large bandana handkerchief, in which I laid them. They were certainly cute little things and there is no doubt but that they would have been born in the next few days. Pat and I sat down and debated as to what to do with them now that we had them. Should we kill them or take them with us. We did not think that they would live as we did not know how we were going to feed them and then not being born naturally and being exposed to the weather, it was just a gamble. We finally decided to keep them and take them along with us.

"Well Pat, lets get this panther skinned as it is getting late and we have lost a lot of time here." After a short time we got her skinned and we put the young kittens in the skin, with the fur side turned inside, so this is the way we carried the young ones which also kept them warm. But here we had another white elephant on our hands, a lot more weight to carry for the hide and kittens must have weighed at least twenty pounds. I told Pat to take the two packs and I would carry the hide and kittens. It was sure funny as it seemed we would only go a short distance and we would have to stop and take look at the kittens. Pat was willing to turn around and head for home but I had made up my mind to go on after the bears.

I won't at this time mention any more about the kittens but later in the story will tell more about them.

We had quite some trouble in picking up the bear tracks again but the dogs seemed to manage very well in bringing us back on the tracks. No doubt you are wondering why we didn't turn Buster loose instead of keeping him back with a rope, but this had to be done so that Ring and Mickie would not get out of sound distance. There is another thing, which I think I mentioned once before, that if Buster was loose, the dogs would have the bear at bay in a few hours but would be impossible to keep up with them, also would be very difficult for us to track the bears in this very rough mountainous country without the dogs to lead us. As we managed to get along on the trail another two or three miles, we decided now was the time to dispose of the doughnuts, and were they ever good but seemed to be a rather light lunch for anyone packing twenty five or thirty pounds for in some places we slid back some ten to fifteen feet and in other places we would have to help each other along, so you see we could not make very good time. But we were both young, stout and healthy, for if we had not been, it would have been impossible for us to have gone on with this trip. I had thought several times during the afternoon about giving up and going home. There seemed to be so much underbrush which was almost impossible to get through in some places and this old panther hide and kittens were three times as heavy now as when I started out with them.

Pat was a good scout, having very little to say and I know of no one else who would have been a better pal to have along with me. We came to many places where we had to make up our minds as to which way to go and I would say to Pat, "Do you want to lead the way." All he would say was, "I am with you, you brought me along on this bear hunt and I am following you."

About the only thing now which made me stick, was that I had been told by several old bear hunters, that when a mother bear is trailed by hunters or dogs, she heads for the roughest of country they can find and I figured that it could not get much rougher than the country we were now in, but if it did, we would have to give it up.

Here is it four o'clock on the second day and maybe you think we were not both tired, seems as though we had been hiking for days and the rifle I was carrying weighed about twenty five pounds but in reality it only weighed about ten or twelve pounds.

"Pat, everything seems to be getting heavier and a little more and I am going to ditch these kittens and the hide, what do you think about it." "Well, lets try to keep them until tonight anyway and by that time they may be dead. We will soon have to find a place for the night as I am so tired and can't go much further."

We had just entered a small grove of pine trees and I noticed that some of the trees had been cut down and made a remark to Pat, "Who in the world do you think has been up in this God forsaken country, cutting these trees down?"

After traveling a short distance, I noticed through the pines, there seemed to be quite an opening, for which we both headed. Here we came to an old picket fence, which was mostly rotted away and there was an old log cabin, which had no doubt been deserted for at least twenty years.

This was surely luck for us as we had to walk through an old apple orchard to get to the cabin and the trees were still loaded with apples but were very small as they had no care or cultivation. We ate some of them and they surely tasted good to us. After we arrived at the cabin and inspected it, we found that it had two rooms but that no one had lived in it for a good many years. There was an old fireplace in one end of the room but was so crumbled down that it took some repairing before we could build a fire in it and while I was doing this, Pat suggested that we use the old cook stove for our cooking but build a fire in the fireplace to keep us warm when we went to bed on the floor.

As I started out to rustle some wood, what should I see at the other end of the orchard, but three deer, a doe and two bucks. I hurried back to the cabin, picking up one of the guns and rushed out of the door asking Pat to come over and let me rest my rifle on his shoulder, which he did. I picked out the largest buck and took dead aim, bringing down the buck with the first shot. We surely had one good feed that night of venison, also seeing that the dogs had their share.

Our next problem was what are we going to do with these kittens and what and how are we going to feed them. We had some eagle brand milk with us, so I suggested that we mix a small quantity of this with some water and try to feed them, but the next thing was, how to do it. I asked Pat if he had a clean white handkerchief with him and he said, "Sure, but what are you going to do with it?" "Well, you just hand it over to me and we will do a bit of experimenting with it right now."

I tore off a small piece of it and made a nipple of it, about the size of a match, dipped it in the milk and put it in the kittens mouth and the little things seemed to know just what to do, so in this way, we fed them and it worked perfectly. They managed to get down about a spoonful but I had very little faith that we would save them until we arrived home for we had no way to take the proper care of them.

"Now Pat, as it is getting dark, you better rustle the wood for the fire place while I cut the deer up and get the rest hung up and if it gets real cold tonight, there will be some good eating for us and it is a cinch that I am going to fry eight or ten slices of the venison for us take with us tomorrow."

I made the remark when we came up to the cabin, "What in the world would make a person come to a place like this to live," and Pat spoke up, "I have been wondering the same thing, what are we doing up here and I think that if we can find a good trail out of here in the morning, we had better be making tracks for home. You do not realize how far we are away from Dyerville."

"I know that we are not very far from the North Fork of the Eel River, which will be our best bet to follow back and did you notice the stream, which we were following, played out a long way down the mountain? I actually think that we are on the summit and if we come to any streams in the morning, they will be flowing the other way. I am sure that the bear and cubs are not too far away but I am afraid I made a mistake of shooting the deer for the report of the gun will carry at least two miles in these mountains. Reason will teach you though that those little cubs will have to rest as it is rough traveling for them in this kind of rough country. No doubt but that we will have some difficulty in finding their trail in the morning."

We finally decided it was time that we get some rest, so we placed our blankets on the floor in front of the fireplace and once more got stretched out. It would be impossible to explain how good it was to lay down and relax even if it was on the floor. We had no more than dozed off when Pat woke up and said, "There must be fleas here for I feel some on me." It wasn't long until I discovered that it was true and the only thing that we could figure out, was that they were Redwood fleas in this old cabin and as we had no light with us, we just turned over and let them bite and our nights sleep and rest was surely broken between the fleas and coyotes and was nearly out of the question to sleep but neither the pests or coyotes seemed to bother the dogs as they were so tired. There is no question in my mind as to why there were so many coyotes, they had smelled the fresh killed deer meat and there is no doubt that if there had been any mountain lions around, they would have been there to help themselves to the fresh meat as there was no door on the back room of the cabin where the meat was hung. We were not afraid of a lion attacking us so long as there was fresh meat for them but just the same it would not be fun to see one enter that room. It certainly makes the chills run down your back when one of these lions or panthers lets out one of their blood curdling screams. Sounds like a terrified scream of a woman. That is when you long for the protection of home.

We were up before daylight the next morning, putting some kindling on the fire in the fireplace so we could see what we were doing. We had venison for breakfast, which we certainly relished. As we were getting our packs ready, we were still arguing as to whether we should take the kittens along with us as this package was so bunglesome to carry. I was ready to dispose of them but Pat could not see it that way, so carry them we did.

I suggested that we go on a right angle from the cabin as we would save quite some distance. After going a short way, we picked up the bear trail which went toward the apple orchard, so we knew that she had gotten a feed of apples and sure enough she had gone to the far end of the orchard, within two hundred feet of where I had shot the deer the night before. At just what time she had been there, I could not tell but it had not been long before we came to the cabin the night before. From this point she turned and went back over her same tracks until she get into the pines again, then took a due course north, right down the mountain side. She had found a deer trail and kept to this until she had reached the bottom of the canyon. We had it much easier, going down grade and after arriving at the bottom of the canyon, there was quite a stream flowing into the North Fork of the Eel River and here we could see that they had had quite a stay and probably taken a good bath. The bears had crossed the stream and so we worked our way up and down the stream, trying to find a place to cross without wading but found no place, so off with our boots and pants and into the shallowest place we could find, and was it ever cold, just like melted ice. After getting across the stream, we must have tracked her for about two miles and at this point she took up a very steep ledge, which was about six to eight hundred feet to the top. This didn't look so good to either of us but at this time we could hear the two small dogs barking as loud as they could.

No doubt they had cornered her and Buster, the dog we had on the rope, was very excited and was so hard to hold back that I thought I had better turn him loose and was sure that he would go no further than where the two other dogs were, so I took the rope from his neck and let him go and I thought he would break his neck going up that steep rocky cliff and I knew that there was no chance for us to follow his trail so we decided to go back down stream for a distance of about five hundred feet as there was another small stream coming down there and by taking this stream, we could make our way up this ridge. We could still hear the dogs making plenty of noise and this encouraged us to speed up as we were so anxious to get there but I finally made up my mind that we would have to cut out the fast traveling or we would not last long and we would sit down every few hundred feet to take a rest. We took turns in carrying the hide and kittens and one thing we were thankful for, was that we had plenty of cold water to drink which kept us pepped up.

We had traveled up this stream for about half a mile and at this place we turned from the stream and took an eastern course and maybe you think we didn't get into some tough climbing. We were going through Manzanita brush so thick that at times we had to drop to our hands and knees and crawl but never-the-less we were getting closer and after working our way through this for a short way, we came to a small opening and what did we see here but a large covey of grouse but did not dare to shoot as we were too close to the dogs and their cornered prey.

"Pat, I do not think we are over five hundred feet from the dogs, so I believe we had better leave our packs and the kittens here on this large rock. There will be no chance of losing them in this opening." After placing our packs on the lower ledge of the rock, I climbed to the top which I should say was about forty feet high and here I had a wonderful view and just a short distance away, I could see the mother bear but not the cubs.

"Come up here Pat if you want to see something." The bear was sitting on her haunches and the dogs were running around her nipping at her and she would make a jump at them but sometimes she would hit at them. Ring and Mickie seemed to get out of her way very easily as they were both small and very quick but Buster was rather clumsy and tired. While we sat there taking a good look all at once she hit Buster and over the cliff he went. This did not look good to me.

"Pat, we must work up within a closer range as there is no danger of her bothering us as long as the two dogs have her cornered, for we could not hit our mark from here."

We worked our way up behind the small trees and rocks and I should say within about one hundred feet from her. Here we sat down and watched for a few minutes, trying to decide our best move. As my gun was of a larger caliber than Pat's, I thought it would be best for me to take the first shot. We made our way a little closer when I told Pat, "I am going to aim directly at her head and if I miss you better be ready to shoot because a grizzly bear is very hard to kill, so here goes." Taking a direct aim off of a limb, my first bullet found its mark but when it hit the bears head, it glanced off, taking some of the hide with it, as we found out later. But oh boy, she surely did feel that. She raised up on her hind feet and made a loud bawl and by this time she had located where the shot came from and started to make her way directly toward us. I then took aim at her heart and shot five times, but she still came on toward us. I then looked for Pat as I wanted him to shoot, as my gun was empty but was no where in sight. He must have run back several hundred feet and I began to think it was time for me to make a move and while running I was trying to get some more shells in my gun and finally got several in the magazine and as I climbed upon the large rock, I looked back and discovered that she had fallen. I really had a hard time to get Pat to come back with me, to see if I had killed her. We were within a few feet of where she had fallen, when we found out that she was not yet dead. It is quite a common occurrence that when a grizzly is shot and just before death, they seem to get renewed strength for their last fight for life. Of course when we approached her, we came from the rear, so if she did try to attack us, it would make it harder for her to locate us. I had only said a few words to Pat, when all at once she made a spring and stood up on her hind feet and by this time we were making tracks back through the brush but she did not get far until she fell again. We then came a little closer and could see that she was taking her last breath. To be sure we did not go up and pat her on the head for several minutes. Finally getting up enough courage, I went up close to her and began to examine her as to how many bullets had hit her and as I mentioned before the first bullet I fired at her head did very little damage. I raised up one of her front legs and found out that most of the bullets had hit her through the heart, or close to it. During this time I did not seem excited or nervous but after it was all over, I was surely weak and shaky.

I told Pat that I had never seen such a large bear in all my life and the next thing to do, was to find the two cubs. Of course it is one of the bear traits, if she has cubs, to hide them if she thinks that there is danger around. Just a few feet from where we had killed her was a tall fir tree. I suggested to Pat that he climb up and get the cub but the tree was too large and was out of the question, so the only way to do it was to shoot the cub, which I did. Upon examining the poor little thing, we found out that it was a female cub I had killed. I hated killing this little fellow for it would have been easy to have kept it for a pet, if there had been any way of getting it down out of that tree. I told Pat that we would get a fifty dollar bounty for it also. So as we were sitting there looking at the little cub, we heard the two dogs barking again and they had treed the other little cub. We made haste to get there and this little fellow had climbed to the first limb of a tree about fifty feet and this tree was a size one could climb and as I felt sorry that I had killed its mate, I made up my mind to climb up there and bring this one down alive.

I got a piece of rope from our pack, pulled off my boots and up the tree I started. Now as I was rather weak and nervous from the foregoing events, I thought several times that I could never make it up to the first limb where the cub was but finally managed to make it to the first limb but things did not look so good when I got up there close to the cub. His claws looked very sharp and I knew I could not go right in and pick him up, so the best thing to do was to lasso him and this was a pretty ticklish job, up in the air fifty feet and out on a limb which was not too large. While trying to get this rope around his neck, he made a strike at me with his front paw and caught me on the wrist of my right hand, his claw making a gash about an inch and half long and all the way to the bone. This surely hurt and I was wishing I had a good pair of buckskin gloves. Now there was only one way to get him down and that was, tie his front paws together so he could not claw me again. The next thing to do was to get something over his mouth so he could not bite me and this was quite a difficult thing to do. I took the other end of the rope and made a loop in it and finally managed to get it around his front paws. I then stood up, hanging on to a smaller limb above me and threw the rope over the same limb to which I was holding and by doing this the cub had to stand up on his hind feet, with his front feet tied together and up in the air but I did not yet have the situation in hand as he could still bite. His teeth were not very large but just like saw teeth. After tying him firmly in this manner, the only thing I could figure out was to pull my shirt off and tear one of the sleeves out which I tied around his mouth and in this way I was able to get hold of him. During all of this time, Pat was standing below me, telling me what to do. I lost my temper several times and told him what I thought of him. "It is mighty fine to stand down there and tell me what to do, especially when there is a bear here beside me."

The cub was not so large but very strong and as he had cut my wrist, I was a little afraid of him and up to this day I still have the scar on my wrist.

Well the bear and I were not out of the tree yet and both of us standing on this limb. If I only had about seventy feet of rope with which I could let him down to the ground but since I did not have it, the only way to do it was to carry him down on my back. I finally managed to get him close to the trunk of the tree where I could get a better hold of him then by taking the rope I had thrown over the upper limb, I tied his hind feet together, then by maneuvering I finally got him on my back with the rope which tied his front feet and hind feet together over my neck or in front of my shoulders, making most of the weight of the bear on the upper part of my back. I was not afraid of falling as I could reach more than half way around the tree trunk but I was afraid that the cub would work loose and if he did it would just be too bad. I started down the tree and it was surely hard on my feet as I had no boots on. I really believe the cub knew I was taking him down out of the tree or else he was too frightened, as he made no struggle to get loose.

Was I ever glad to get down on the ground as my wrist was bleeding very bad where I had been cut by the bears claws. I tore a piece of my shirt off and tied up the wound. I have always figured that I was mighty lucky in not getting infection from the claws but I think that the only thing that prevented it was that it bled so freely.

"Well Pat, you will have to put on my boots and lace them for me as I am all-in, but I'll be all right in a few minutes." After resting for a short time, I got a stick about six or seven feet long and put it through the rope, which tied both front and hind feet of the bear and we carried him back to where we had killed the mother bear and other cub. We untied his feet and took the shirtsleeves from around his mouth and tied him to a tree near by.

He was a cute little fellow and it didn't take long to make friends with him and he did not seem to realize that we had killed his mother and sister.

"Pat, as it is getting late, I think that you had better go take a look for Buster as he has not come in yet and in the meantime, I will fix up a bite to eat." We had been so excited that we had forgotten all about lunch and here it was nearly four o'clock.

"Now you work fast and do not be gone over an hour and do be careful about getting on that shale as it is very dangerous and will break off very easily and let you go to the bottom of the canyon."

We still had the deer meat which I had cooked and had intended to have for lunch, so it did not take me long to get us a very good feed and it was not over twenty five minutes until Pat returned without Buster and told me that he was dead. He had landed on a ledge of rock some distance below the cliff where we had seen the mother bear knock him over. This made me feel pretty blue as the dog did not belong to me and he was valued at five hundred dollars.

After finishing our meal, I thought it best to draw the bear and cub and this was quite some job as it was the first bear I had ever killed. When I got her opened up, I discovered that two of the bullets had plowed through the center of her heart and two others a distance of a few inches, the fifty bullet must have gone wild. We had to do all of this with the bear lying on her back as it was out of the question to try to move her or hang her up. We hung the cub up while we skinned her and also thought we might want a piece of bear meat the next day.

All of a sudden Pat jumped up and said, "My we have forgotten all about those poor little kittens, I'll bet they are dead this time." Pat ran down to where we had left them on the rock and was back with them in a hurry. Now we were gathering quite a menagerie, with our cub and panther kittens. Pat fixed some milk for the poor little things and did they ever devour it and after feeding them, he again wrapped them good for the night.

We had to cut down some brush on which we spread our blankets and after fixing a good fire, we once more took off our boots and stretched out for a rest which we surely needed. We then began to realize the danger we might be taking in going to sleep at all with the carcasses of both the mother bear and cub so near camp. Of course we had some protection with the two small dogs as they would warn us if any wolves or other animals came into camp.

As I lay there, I tried to figure out what was our next move in the morning for I knew we were a long way from Dyerville. I suggested to Pat that we build a small raft on which we could easily take the cub, bear hides, panther hide and kittens, also the two dogs. I finally got so sleepy that I could not finish so wandered into dreamland.

During the night we were disturbed several times by the cub trying to get loose but he found it was useless and finally went to sleep himself.

We were up bright and early the next morning and found everything all okay with our menagerie all intact and hungry. I stirred the camp fire the first thing so as to get some warm water to fix the milk for the kittens and say did they enjoy this and seemed to be getting along fine. The next joker on our hands was the cub, what will he eat as he was still nursing the mother so we thought the best thing was to try him on some milk. He took a little but was not satisfied with it. As we had cooked some of the bear meat for the dogs, we gave some of it to him and he seemed to enjoy it. It didn't seem to make any difference what kind of meat it was, as he was hungry. You know the old saying, "Hungry as a Bear" and to tell the truth I think we were all hungry as a bear.

By the time the kittens, dogs, cub and ourselves had our breakfast, it was time to decide what was our next step to take as I had given up the idea of making a raft and try to go down the river so I suggested to Pat that he stay here in the camp and I would walk back up the ridge to see if I could locate a road or trail which we could take out. After I had hiked about half a mile, I discovered a cabin with smoke coming from the chimney and this was no doubt about two miles away. I hurried back to Pat and told him what I had found and that I thought it was best for me to try and make my way down there as we might be able to get some help.

I started out and left the two dogs in camp with Pat and told him I was sure I would not be over three or four hours. I had not traveled very far when I came to an old cow trail which lead almost directly to the log cabin and after arriving at the cabin, I was very fortunate in finding that it was the home of a half breed Indian. He told me that I was very lucky in finding him in his cabin as in another few minutes he would have been out on the range. I introduced myself to him and explained that my mother ran the hotel at Dyerville and he said that he was very well acquainted with her. To my recollection, he said that his name was Hawks. I then told him about killing the two bears and the mountain lion and that we had one of the cubs alive and also the kittens. He seemed to be very much interested and wanted to know if I had had any breakfast, I told him what I had eaten and he kind of smiled and wanted to know if I didn't think I could eat again and when I looked over at the table I saw several dozen eggs in a bowl, so I said, "I think I can get away with a few of those eggs soft boiled and may I take a few of them back to Pat."

"Sure you can, I also have some stew here which we will take along for our lunch. It is made with jerky and I think you will like it. At least it will stick to our ribs and give us strength for our work we have to do."

After I had finished eating the eggs, Mr. Hawks said that as soon as we could get ready we will start out to our camp but first he had something out in front of his cabin he wanted to show me. I could not imagine what it could be but I went along with him. We had not gone very far when we came upon two graves. He said he had buried his mother there several years ago and in the other grave was his sister who had passed away recently. I felt very sorry for him as he was so far back in these mountains. He was not a poor man as he owned several thousand head of sheep and also several hundred head of cattle. I really did not understand how he could stay up there by himself and get any enjoyment out of life. His closest neighbor was about five miles away but he said he went to Eureka and San Francisco once or twice a year, spending a week or two at a time. He seemed to have a good education.

"Well I think I have a couple horses here which will go close to the bear as these horses have been around wild animals before. As I get the horses saddled, you get one of those sharp axes over there on the wood pile, also I think we better take plenty of rope and some of that whang hanging up over there."

We were soon on our way back to camp where Pat was waiting. It was a pleasure to be riding horse instead of hiking and took us but a short time to get to camp and when Pat saw us, there was a smile on his face as Pat had met Mr. Hawks before, so they were not strangers.

The horses got the scent of the bear and began to shy but Mr. Hawks tied them to a tree so they could not run away. I then took him over and showed him the mother bear, he seemed quite surprised and said, "Well, well this is a Silver Tip Grizzly, they are sure scarce in this country. This is the first I know of to be killed in this part of the country for at least six or eight years." He stood there looking at her head and said, "I am sure she is at least fifteen or sixteen years old as she has considerable gray on the top of her nose as that is about the best way to tell how old they are and you have no doubt saved me several head of cattle and sheep as it is not uncommon for a grizzly to kill several head in a few months."

I then asked him to come over and see our small panther kittens as I explained to him how we had saved them and he got quite a kick out of this and said, "Well there are several more head of sheep saved and I will say that I have my doubts as to your being able to raise them for they are so young."

Pat had the little cut eating out of his hand and playing with him and of course we had to go see him too and pass opinion as to what we would do with him.

Mr. Hawks then went over to where the horses were tied and brought one over close to the bear and then told me to bring the other horse over, which I did and he made both horses come within a few feet of the mother bear which was hard to do but he said that was the only thing to do as he had to get them used to the bear. They did not seem to get very frightened of the little cub.

I asked him just how far it was over to the main road and he said it was about thirteen miles by wagon road and eight by horse trail. "Do you think it would be possible to take the mother bear back to Dyerville just as she is?"

"No, I think the best thing to do is to skin her here and leave the carcass here as she will take up so much room and is too heavy." "I know it, but I'd like to take her back just as she is without being skinned as I want to weigh her and then too I want to show some of those fellows what I killed."

"I think she will weigh around a thousand pounds, but it is up to you, I think we could probably get her to my wagon road trail which is about one and a half miles away and mostly down grade. I could then get my wagon and load her into it."

"Well can you tell me just about how much this will cost me to get the mother bear, cub, kittens and baggage back to Dyerville?"

He gave me a funny look and said, "Why you have saved me several hundred dollars by killing these animals and I would not think of charging you a cent."

Mr. Hawks then proceeded to get a couple limbs and cross limbs tied together on which he helped me place the mother bear, it took us about an hour until we had the bear loaded. It was quite a puzzle as to how was the best way to get her on as she was so heavy but Mr. Hawks tied a rope on to the neck of the bear and to one of the saddle horns and in this way pulled the bear carcass upon this rack he had built. We had plenty of rope and whang to tie her with and we then took the panther hide in which the kittens were wrapped and also the hide of the other cub and tied them to the horn of the other saddle.

I then cut a small pole about eight feet long and tied the cub in the center of it, giving him about a foot of rope and then gave the other end of the pole to Pat, I figured by doing this the cub could not get to either of us to bite us or scratch us for I knew he was not going to like being lead this way.

It was remarkable how the horses carried the bear on those two poles, which were fastened to either side of the saddle, especially over this rough country. Mr. Hawks lead this horse and did not go very far at a time until he would rest the horse. Pat and I followed leading the other horse and also the cub in between us. I have often thought, since the invention of motion pictures, what a sight this would have been and we did not even get a snap shot as we did not bring a camera with us. I judge we were an hour or more in getting to the old wagon trail. Even this old wagon trail looked good to us. Mr. Hawks said we would then hitch the team to the wagon and we would then load the bear into the wagon.

Pat did not seem much in favor of this as he did not want to leave the cub and kittens there but we finally tied the cub to a tree with some of the whang but took the kittens on down to the house with us so we could feed them some fresh milk and did they ever enjoy it and we all got such a kick out of feeding them with a little piece of cloth.

Mr. Hawks said he had an old bird cage which he would look up and that it would be just the thing for us to carry them down the mountain.

We then had our lunch, which consisted of plenty of rich sweet milk and butter, jam and a large amount of jerky stew, oh, boy did it ever taste good. Both Pat and I really done justice to this meal and really felt guilty as we must have drank eight or ten glasses of milk but Mr. Hawks seemed to be so pleased that we enjoyed it so much.

After lunch Mr. Hawks found the old bird cage in which we put the kittens wrapped in some warm cloth. We then went to the barn and hitched the team to the wagon and were on our way back to where we left the cub and mother bear.

Pat said, "I did not forget the little cub, see what I have in my pocket for him, three apples and I bet he will go for them too."

When we got to where we had left the cub and mother bear, we found the poor little cub had wound himself all around the tree and seemed so glad to see us and he certainly did enjoy those apples Pat brought for him.

Mr. Hawks said that it would make it very late if we tried to make it to Dyerville that night and he thought it best for us to go as far as the overland road and stay there with some friends of his and go into Dyerville the next morning. I was very pleased with this arrangement too.

It did not take long in loading the bear into the wagon as we unhitched the team or rather the doubletree and placed a rope around it and then to the poles and pulled the bear and all just as it was upon the wagon with the poles sticking over the front of the wagon about five feet which Mr. Hawks cut off with the ax, so that it fit right down into the wagon bed.

Now a pitiful thing happened when we were all ready, we put the little cub in the wagon close to his mother and he knew there was something wrong as he began to whine like a dog but there was nothing we could do so we finished loading the cub hide, panther hide, bird cage with the kittens, and the two dogs. By this time the circus was ready to move on down the mountain. I cannot explain how I felt when we were all in the wagon and on our way towards home.

I was so proud to think that I had killed a grizzly bear and really taking it home with me as proof for these fellows who had given us the horselaugh when we left. No doubt but that my mother had worried a great deal since we left as this was our fourth day away and she had heard nothing from us.

Everything went along fine from there on and we arrived at the friends of Mr. Hawks, where we spent the night. These people were white, their names being Sylvester and they surely did give us a fine welcome.

I had no more than gotten off the wagon, when Mr. Sylvester asked what was wrong with my wrist and I explained how the cub had cut it with his claw. He told me to come right into the house and informed me that he was a doctor for that vicinity in the mountains. He at once took off the bandage and cleaned the wound, then cauterizing it and after that took six stitches.

He said I was mighty lucky not to have an infection in it as he was sure the bear claws were poisonous. I then told him who I was and where I lived and he said he was very well acquainted with my mother and he then suggested that I call my mother on the telephone and let her know that we were both safe and would see her in the morning.

I called my mother immediately and explained to her just where we were and that we were okay and would be home in the morning and she was so glad to hear my voice as she said she had been so worried for she was sure that something had happened to me and she was so pleased to hear of our success. I had thought I'd keep the bear a secret but I could not as it was too good to keep. She told me that if we had not returned by the next day she had planned to send some Indian trackers out after us for everyone was sure that something had gone wrong. She said she was so glad we had called as now she would get a good nights sleep, which she had not done since we left. I told mother that was one thing I wanted to do myself, get some rest and I would see her in the morning.

While talking with Mr. Sylvester, telling him of my experience with the panther kittens and bears, he suggested that it would be best for me to get a house cat which had small kittens and dispose of them and put the panther kittens with the cat and he was sure in that way we could raise them all right. He had no more mentioned this than Mrs. Sylvester said that a friend of theirs in Garberville owned a cat who had just had a litter of kittens the previous week. She said she would call them and see if it would be possible to get the cat for me. It was pretty late by this time but she succeeded in getting them and told them what she wanted. I told her to tell them that I would be willing to buy the cat if they would sell her, but they said I was welcome to have her until the kittens were large enough to feed themselves. The next question was how we were to get the cat to us. Mrs. Sylvester told them that the best way would be for them to put the cat in a box and get it on the next stage, which came through Garberville at eleven o'clock. It was then about nine thirty p.m. so they had plenty of time.

The stage, for some reason, was several hours late and we did not receive the cat and her kittens, which they had put in with the mother cat, until much later the next morning. We took the kittens away from the mother cat disposing of them and placed the baby panther kittens in with her and it only took the baby panther kittens a few minutes until they were nursing and the mother cat was washing them as though they were her own.

"Well Mr. Hawks, I think that it is time that we were getting on our way to Dyerville as I am afraid the old mother bear will not keep much longer as we have had a couple of warm days although the nights have been real cold but I do want to get her home in good condition."

We were not long in getting everything loaded again and ready to start on the last leg of our journey. We thanked Mr. and Mrs. Sylvester for their hospitality and kindness to us and started on our way home.

The stage road was narrow and very rough and when we arrived in the big redwood forest close to the Eel River, the ruts in the road had worn down to the roots of the trees. In some places these roots stood up as high as six or eight inches and it certainly made it very uncomfortable riding and I think a person would enjoy walking much more than riding over these roots in the wagon. It was not quite so rough riding in the stages over these rough roads as the stages were mounted on leather rockers or springs, but there were no rockers or springs on Mr. Hawks wagon.

A few hours later we arrived at the Eel River where we had to cross on the ferry boat and there was another team and wagon waiting for the ferry to come back across and as soon as it arrived the man who runs the ferry came up to us and took a look at our circus and said that he could not take us on this trip across as he had this other team to take over and that the horses might get frightened if he put both of us on at the same time and that they might jump off the ferry so we had to wait until he made the round trip. Of course the ferryman had to advertise to the people in Dyerville, which was just across the river that we were back with a bear and the whole inhabitance of the town was at the ferry to meet us when we got across.

This was one of the greatest days of my life, I was so proud and I think I had a right to be too as there were not many men who had brought back the first grizzly they went after. Also I had brought a cub and four panther kittens and both the hides of the mother panther and cub bear. About this time I looked up and saw Mr. Carlton, now this made me feel so bad as I had to explain to him about Buster getting killed. Of course he felt very bad about it, but after giving him full details of the whole situation, he became reconciled to the loss of his great bear dog Buster. Both the other dogs, Ring and Mickie were surely glad to see him

Mr. Hawks then drove from the ferry landing over to the front of the hotel where we unloaded part of our circus, taking the little cub off first. He was becoming very friendly with us so it was not too hard to lead him about. I found a small chain, with which I chained him to an apple tree out in front of the hotel. We then unloaded the kittens and mother cat, these we put in the wood shed.

My mother said, "Well, Frank do you think you are going to turn this hotel into a zoo? I can't have all these animals around here, the people will not stand for it and besides they will be afraid of the bear."

"Now mother, I think it will be an advertisement for the hotel as we can have a cage out in front with the wild animals in it."

"Well we will settle this later, you go get that wagon unloaded."

I then went back to the wagon, and there I found three or four stage drivers, a couple of horse back riders and a few other men, all were examining the mother bear and there were plenty of arguments as to what kind of a grizzly bear she was, but finally all agreed that she was a Silver Tip Grizzly.

One old fellow, who worked at the blacksmith shop, called to me, "Well Frank what are you going to do with that bear."

"I intend to hang her up and skin her and then render out the fat and any one who wishes bear meat to eat are welcome to help themselves."

We got a large timber and placed it on top of the barn and blacksmith shop and then took a small block and tackle and fastened to the center of this timber, hoisting the bear up as we always did with a thousand pound beef to skin and dress. Oh yes, before we did this, we weighed the wagon and bear as I wanted so much to know just what she weighed and it was one thousand seventeen pounds. Of course we had plenty of help as all the people who lived around Dyerville seemed to live the life of leisure, and they were all there to see and to help if we needed them. We had a very hard time getting the bear skinned as she had been killed for several days and the hide was so tough but after sharpening all the butcher knives on the place we finally succeeded. There was an enormous amount of fat, which we cut out and put into wash tubs, dish pans and anything else we could find. I then took these over to the back of the hotel where we had a large black iron kettle, in which we boiled the clothes for washing, after cleaning thoroughly, I put all the fat into this kettle and built a fire under it and in this way we rendered out the lard. My mother had used bear lard for pasty and she considered it better than hog lard. It was not so good for frying though.

There was nearly twenty gallons of this lard when rendered. The meat was cut up and divided up among all the neighbors and any one who happened to be there. Some of the meat was served at the hotel that night for dinner but I cannot say it was delicious as it was so tough and I could not eat it. There was quite a laugh all over the village as most every one had bear meat for dinner and all found out it could not be eaten. I think it would have been easier to eat the sole of your shoes as to try to eat a piece of this meat.

Mrs. Carland came over right after dinner and sprung a good joke on us, saying that the meat they had for dinner was surely fine but the bear meat she had given to the dogs and that they were still chewing on it. Mr. Hawks spoke up, saying that the bear was too old, that she was at least twenty years old. Mrs. Carland said she was sure that he had made a mistake, that it certainly must have been fifty years old. After we decided the bear meat could not be eaten, we put it through a meat grinder and fed it to the chickens and the hogs. This worked out all okay until I put some through which was so tough it broke the grinder. This reminds me of some of the meat we buy today which is supposed to be corn fed baby beef, which never ever had a look at a grain of corn.

The next day, the hotel had a big business run, we must have fed at least fifty people. They came from all the small towns around the country to see the mother bear hide, cub and panther kittens. They were too late to see the mother bear, as there was nothing left of her but hide and carcass. There were several full blooded Indians as well as several half breeds to whom I even sold some of the bear teeth.

This was a great day in Dyerville, I had never seen half as many people in town at one time. It was the general rule in this country, that when the Indians or ranchers came into town on a special occasion as this, they would stay two or three days or until all of their money was spent. The hotel, mercantile store, saloon and gambling hall reaped the benefits.

"Now mother, I think our zoo has already started to bring in business to the hotel, for really you have taken in more money in the last three days than you have for two weeks." All mother could say was, "Guess you are right, but just the same I am not crazy about having these animals here."

The saloon keeper said that he had to put on an extra bartender, also that if this kept up another day or so, he would be all out of beer and whiskey.

Mr. Hawks only stayed a day or so with us as he had to get back to his ranch. I suggested to the merchants of Dyerville that I thought it nothing but right that they all pitch in and make up a purse for Mr. Hawks, as he was the one who had made it possible for me to get the bear back to town, thus bringing all this crowd here to spend their money but Mr. Hawks would not listen to this as he said he had been as much benefited by the killing of the mother bear and panther and probably more than any of the rest. He was such a good fine specimen of half breed Indian, most accommodating and willing to help and when he left he invited me up to his ranch for a visit and I promised him that I would remember.

Pat and I took turns in caring for the baby panthers as we were so anxious for their eyes to open and the old mother cat seemed to be perfectly contented with them for she treated them just as though they were her own babies. It was about two weeks later that Pat discovered that the kittens eyes were opening. He was so excited and it seemed as though he spent most of his time with them or else with the cub bear, which had been christened Buster, after the dog who had been killed on the trip and you could always bet you would find him at one place or the other.

When the baby panthers began to eat food they grew very rapidly and was not long until they were larger than their adopted mother and after the mother cat had weaned the kittens, they drank a great deal of milk and if I remember right, they were about two months old before they ate bread and meat. They played a great deal, but it did not sound like play as it sounded more like fighting, sometimes all of them in it at once and the older they grew, the more vicious they became and you were never sure just what their next move would be as they were great to make quick jumps. I tried to keep them tame so I could pet them as they were certainly pretty things. One of their habits was to make faces at any one who came near them. They were great pets but so much trouble as they did not like to be caged up and liked their freedom. Several old hunters advised me that it would be out of the question to do anything with them after they had reached the age of six months and that I had better dispose of them for they would hurt me. I remember one evening I took the four kittens into the office of the hotel as there were no guests in there and I let them play around while I read the paper and I had not noticed that one of the kittens had jumped on the mantel of the old fireplace and all at once the kitten landed right in my face but I had the paper up in front of my face which protected me. He tore the paper all to bits but did not hurt me in any way but surely frightened me plenty. He had jumped at least twelve feet and right there and then I made up my mind that the party who had told me to dispose of these kittens was right, so the next day I wrote a letter to the Sheriff and it was but a few days until I received word that he would come or send someone to get the four baby panthers, allowing me two hundred dollars for them as the bounty would have been that amount. I put them into a box and had them ready for the trip to their new home, which was to be a zoo located in the county seat. I surely hated to see them go but knew it was best as their claws were so long and sharp, also their teeth were just like knives when they would bite, which they were constantly doing if you touched one of them.

Now getting back to the story of the bear, Buster the Silver Tip Grizzly, as he was now called. He made friends with everyone but sometimes he would get very rough with them.

I remember of one funny instance, which happened after I had him for about three months. My brother and I planned to take him in the woods for a stroll to see how he would act. We tied a rope on his collar, leaving two long ends to which my brother and myself held, so he could not get to either of us and kept well in the center of the path. He had not been taught to lead, so I think he was dragged more than lead. Anyway we finally got him down to the river and by that time he was getting very angry. We thought it would be fun to take him in a boat and cross the river so after getting him into the boat which was no easy task as he was growling and scratching all the time, in other words he was getting real mean and did not like the idea of the boat. I was in the front end of the boat and dragged Buster in after me and just then my brother turned loose of the rope and as Buster was so made for me dragging him into the boat, that he tackled me, grabbing me around the waist, beginning to squeeze me. To my recollection, Buster weighed about one hundred fifty pounds and was about three and a half feet high, so he was quite strong although he was not large enough to hurt me, I did not like the feeling of those front paws of his around me so tight. I knew I had to do something, but what I didn't just know, I tried to get hold of his collar but he would bite me so I called to my brother who was standing on the bank enjoying himself at my expense, to please pull Buster off as he was tearing my clothes. He then made an attempt to help me but in so doing, Buster and I seemed to get on the same side of the boat, so over it went and both Buster and myself were in the water and this was not so funny as Buster was holding on to me but as the water was only two or three feet deep, I managed to get away from him. Well we did not try to get him into the boat again and we were mighty glad to get him back to the hotel safely tied up again.

After this experience, I made it a habit to take him out every day and lead him around in the yard and also started to train him to do little stunts. He soon became very attached to me and knew his name so well that when I turned him loose, he would come when I called him. The first trick I taught him to was to stand on his head. This was rather difficult as he was so young and he always wanted to play. I always gave him a piece of candy or apple after he tried to do the trick and he finally knew what I was trying to have him do.

One day while my mother was hanging up some clothes on the clothes line, she dropped some of the clothes pins on the ground and as it happened, the line was in the same yard in which Buster was chained. There was a large Redwood stump on which Buster liked to sit, close to the clothes line and as my mother was bending over to pick up the pins, Buster made a dive and landed right on mothers back and making a noise. This of course scared my mother so bad that she went right in to the hotel and getting a double barreled shot gun was going out to kill Buster but as it happened Pat met her and asked her what she was going to do with the gun and she said, "Well I am going to kill that bear, he nearly killed me. I knew if we kept him around here he would kill someone, he might just have well killed me for he scared me to death." Pat had to do some talking to get the gun away from her for I know she would have killed him. I was not at the hotel when this happened and when I came back, mother told me all about it, still saying that Buster would have to be killed or else sent away. I certainly had a good laugh but mother could not see the funny side to it. Finally mother said I would have to build a cage to keep him in but I was sure Buster must have taken her for a dog, as he did not seem to make up with dogs, she let me leave him where he was.

On several occasions, I had tried to have him make up with different dogs around there but it was out of the question to get one close enough to him. He would start out on a run toward them and as soon as they came anywhere near him, the dog would beat it. I did not blame the dog for getting out of his way for I imagine he would have treated the dog pretty rough had he gotten hold of him. I have known black or cinnamon bears to make up with dogs and have them for pals, but Buster was of a different temperment.

Buster soon became used to having the people come up close to him and try to make friends with him, most would try to feed him, thus Buster spent a great deal of his time eating. Besides all that was fed to him by the people of the village and guests of the hotel and all or most of the scraps from the hotel, this was the reason he grew so fast, it seemed to me as though he gained at least a pound a day.

One day the wind was blowing quite a gale and one of the stage drivers came in and told me that the wind was blowing all the shingles off the barn so I went out and looking across the road to where the barn stood, what do you think I saw, there was Buster on top of the barn tearing the shingles off and watching the wind take them away, he was surely getting a kick out of it. Buster had gotten loose some way and gone across the road and up on the barn. I rushed over there as fast as I could, getting hold of his chain and trying to pull him down but he paid no attention to me and went right on pulling off the shingles. I went into the barn and got a pitchfork, with which I intended to hit him, but not hurt him, so he would get down. But I did hurt him seriously, as it so happened, one of the prongs of the pitch fork was broken off about three inches from the end and as I hit him with it, the broken tine hit him in they eye and tore his eye out. He bawled and whined for quite a while and I surely felt so sorry for him as I thought a lot of Buster.

I managed to get him down from the top of the barn and tied him to an apple tree, I then ran over to the hotel and got a pair of scissors so I could cut the small tendon which was holding the ball of the eye and was hanging down on his check. Up to this day, I have not forgotten this experience. The eye socket healed up in a few weeks and did not seem to be very noticeable but from that time on, Buster was very careful not to let anyone come up on his blind side. I have always wondered why he took such a liking to me, as I was the cause of him being blind. I tried to make it up to him though as I was always very kind to him, although I made it very clear to him that I was not afraid of him. Many times I took away from him whatever he would be eating and he would never growl or make a fuss but seemed to know that I had the right to do it.

The winter rains had begun to fall and it was very wet and muddy and while mentioning the climate at Dyerville, it is true that this particular winter I did not see the sun for fifty days consecutively. It did not rain steady for this length of time but if one stayed outside long enough, you would be wet. This weather did not seem to bother Buster, I really think he liked it and where he would travel back and forth making a half circle, he got so muddy and dirty.

During these long rainy days, there was very little travel by stage so there was not much to be done at the hotel. This gave me plenty of time to spend with Buster so I would take him in the wood shed, where I would train him to do his tricks. I gave him a stick and trained him to march with it, this he did easily but when it came to making him walk on his forepaws, also walk as though he were crippled in one foot, it took considerable time and patience. One of the tricks which took much time was standing on one front paw for five or ten seconds. It took much candy and many apples to get him to do these stunts as well as patience for so much of the time Buster wanted to play. I would of course play with him some of the time but he would get so rough and he did not realize how strong he was, so it was rather hard to make him understand that he could not hit so hard.

Before the winter was over, I had Buster doing many tricks and I also took him for strolls in the Redwood, sometimes for a quarter of a mile or more. I would never have a leash on him and he would follow with me just like a dog. Some of the trees in the forest are several hundred feet high and Buster would sometimes take a notion to climb one and then it was a bit difficult to get him down but usually if I walked away a short distance he would come down. It seemed he would go as far up the tree as he could go just to tease me.

One day I had him out for a walk and he took a sudden notion to swim the river. I called to him to come back but he paid no attention and kept right on swimming across the river and into the forest, which was very heavy. Of course I thought Buster was gone for sure and I had no way of getting across the river unless I swam so I hurried to the ferry landing and got a row boat and rowed across and when I got over there, I walked up a small stream, and there was Buster coming down stream, headed for home. He had not seen me but guess he realized that I had not followed him as he was in very much of a hurry to get to the hotel. The people of the village had seen him come in all by himself without a chain and that he was all wet. They could not figure out what had happened, so some of them came down to the river to see if I was there and of course saw me coming back in the boat. It showed that if you treat an animal with kindness, they will most always come back where they are raised and taken care of.

As spring was about here again, I was making arrangements to go back to Oklahoma, where my father had started to build a public park, which was near Hobart, Oklahoma and my father was anxious for me to help him with the work of building this park. I hated to leave my mother and pet bear and I would have liked to take Buster with me but he was now weighing over three hundred pounds and it would cost considerable to ship him back to Oklahoma, so I left him at the hotel in the care of my mother.

On my way back to Oklahoma, I got to thinking of Buster, how smart he was and how attached to him I had become, just as a person would to a dog. After arriving in Hobart, I wrote my mother often, of course the main reason was to know how Buster was making it without me. I was very lonesome without him and I was sure that he missed me.

A few months rolled by and during this time, while helping my father build a lake, setting out trees and flowers in this park, I received a letter from my mother, stating that she would have to sell Buster or dispose of him some way as she was afraid that he would hurt some child or person. She also said he was too much of a care for her and he was getting too restless as he would whine at night and this bothered the guests in the hotel. I did not know what to say, I wanted to ship him back to Hobart, but I knew it would cost me about one hundred fifty dollars, as he would have to be shipped by express. This was a great deal of money at that time and as I did not have that amount, I would just have to forget it. I wrote mother telling her that I wished I had him with me but I could not figure out how I could get the money to send for him so she would have to do what she thought best if she could not keep him.

One day I received a letter from my brother-in-law that Buster was being shipped to me by express and as he had been shipped a few days before the telegram was sent, I knew he would arrive in a day or so. Words cannot express how happy I was when I received that message and of course this news spread all over town like wild fire. Hobart had a population of about nine thousand and I think that all knew that Buster the Silver Tip Grizzly was being shipped to me from California. It was surprising how busy I was the next couple of days answering questions about Buster. I would go to meet most of the trains as they came in, to see if Buster was on them but of course I had several disappointments and also went to find out from the agent if he knew just what train he would be on but it seemed he could not give me any information. One morning I happened to be going by the Wells Fargo Express Office, and as I was very well acquainted with the agent, he called me in and told me that he had received the Bill of Lading on the bear which was shipped from California. He also informed me that there was a charge of Two Hundred Dollars against him. Now I cannot explain how I felt when he told me this and I tried to explain to him that there must be some mistake for I was sure all the expenses had been paid and he said that the money had to be paid to Wells Fargo Company before he could turn the bear over to me. I told him I was afraid Wells Fargo Company would have a bear on their hands for I could see no way to raise that amount of money.

This was about nine o'clock in the morning, so I hurried right out to the park where my father was and explained to him just what had happened and I asked him if it would be possible for him to give me enough money to put with what I had, so I could pay the express on Buster. He gave me the amount I asked for and I wasted no time in getting back to town but all the time wondering if Buster was worth Two Hundred Fifty Dollars.

The train, on which Buster was, arrived at three o'clock in the afternoon, but I was there quite some time before the train arrived and I had not yet paid Wells Fargo Company as I wanted to wait until I had seen Buster and also to see if he was okay. About half an hour before the train pulled in, the depot agent came out and said, "Well it looks to me as though your bear would be in today and he certainly is going to get some welcome. Just take a look at the crowd here." There is no doubt but that there was three hundred people at the depot and by the time the train arrived, there must have been close to six hundred. All that was lacking was the City Band. It seemed to me as though the train would never get there but never-the-less it was on time and I was right there beside the express door when the train stopped. The baggage man opened the door of the car and made this remark, "You fellows out there better be hunting a hole to get into as there is a bear in here in a crate and he has gnawed the crate until he is about out." I jumped upon the truck and into the car but the baggage man grabbed me and said, "Young fellow you better look out, that bear has been gnawing that crate and trying to get out ever since I came into this car at Camerillo, Texas. The only way I could get him to stop, was to feed him peaches. I do not know what the Express Company will say, when I tell them that I fed about ten baskets of peaches to this bear."

I explained to him that the bear belonged to me and that I had caught him when he was a little cub. I then examined the crate and sure enough, he did have one of the large timbers gnawed in two and also two more were almost in the same condition. These timbers were about two and one half inches through. I told the baggage man that as the crate was so heavy, I thought it would be a good thing to take Buster out of the crate while he was in the car and I could lead him out and it would not be so hard to remove the crate from the car. The baggage man made this remark, "That bear is not going to be taken out of that crate in this car, at least not while I am in here."

I then invited several men into the car, who were friends of mine to give me some assistance in moving the crate out on the truck. They were willing enough to help me but were so frightened of Buster and as the crate was pretty well damaged, it was no easy job in getting it out. We finally had to get a rope and tie onto the crate and drag it out onto the truck.

"Thank goodness that job is done and if I had any idea that there would ever be another bear shipped in my car, someone else would be welcome to my job." He also said, "I usually get about five hours sleep on my run, but up until now, I have not even had one minute sleep, as it kept me busy watching that bear."

I then noticed that there was a card tacked on the top of the crate and on it was printed, Buster Silver Tip Grizzly, consigned to F.T. Briles, Hobart, Oklahoma. Deadhead, bear must be fed once a day and watered twice each day. I then asked the expressman what the word "deadhead" meant and he informed me that there was to be no charges of express on the bear as all charges had been prepaid. I asked him if he was sure of that as the Wells Fargo Express Company claimed I would have to pay them

Two Hundred Fifty Dollars before they would release him. He said, "Well they might claim it, but do not give them a cent, for it is all paid."

All this time we had taken to unload the bear had delayed the train at least four or five minutes but the engineer, fireman, conductor and all the passengers were watching this procedure of unloading Buster, the conductor made the remark that it was well worth the delay.

The agent for Wells Fargo Company then came up to me and asked me where I wanted the bear delivered. I told him that I intended to take Buster out of the crate and lead him out to the park, which we were just finishing. He then asked me if I had made arrangements for the Two Hundred Fifty Dollars express charges. I told him that I had but that the expressman on the train had told me that the bear had been shipped as deadhead and that all chargers were paid. We had a few words and finally called the depot agent out and I explained to him that the bear had been deadhead and that he could get upon the truck and look at the card which was tacked on the crate, which he did, and he said that there was a Wells Fargo stamp on the deadhead, also a signature of the Express agent in Eureka, California.

The Wells Fargo agent then decided that I could have Buster and as I had told him that there was no use of him hauling Buster out to the Park, that I would take him out of the crate and that he could then take the crate up to the Wells Fargo office and I would call for it later. He said that was alright but just wait until he had his express all loaded on to the wagon.

The people who had come down to see Buster arriver were crowding very close to the hand truck on which Busters cage stood and this made it very difficult to get Buster out of the crate. He still had his collar on in which there was a ring but his chain was not snapped into it. On top of the crate and at one end was the chain in a heavy sack, which had been securely nailed to the crate, so it would not get lost. The depot agent brought me a hammer, so I could get the chain off. In one end of the crate was a door which slid up and down and this had been nailed down with extra heavy nails, also wired to the sides and when I began to pull out the nails which held the door fast, it did not take the crowd long to get back. The night watchman stepped up and asked me if I was sure that the bear was tame enough to take out of the crate right there in that crowd and was I sure that I could control him. I told him I would show him that Buster still knew me and that I was not afraid of him. I then stuck my hand into the crate and petted him on the head, he seemed tickled that I had done it.

As there were so many people watching me take the bear out of this crate, I advised them not to make any strange or loud noise as it might frighten him. I then went ahead with the opening of the door and you should have seen the people scramble. Some climbed upon the top of the depot, others on top of box cars which were close enough for them to see and by the time I got the doors open, I really believe there was no person closer than seventy-five feet of me. I had plenty of room so I took the chain and snapped it in the ring of his collar and petted him on the head, calling him by name several times. I pulled on the chain a little and Buster finally crawled out onto the platform of the truck. He then jumped down onto the board walk and began to smell all around, finally raising on his hind legs, he began to smell all around my face and ears and I knew he remembered me as though I had only been away from him for a few days, now maybe you think that the people were not real quiet, but they were as I had explained to them, if he became excited he might break loose from me and some of them might get hurt. I had no trouble in leading him away from the depot and right through town. As I was leading him along the street, I called a boy over and gave him a dime to get some mixed candy which I wanted to feed to Buster, but the boy never came back. I saw the boy two or three days later and asked him why he did not come back with the candy and he said that after he got to thinking about it he did not want to feed the bear and I told him that I had not intended for him to feed Buster but that I had wanted the candy to feed to Buster myself, so he gave the dime back to me but I made him take it back and told him to buy himself some candy as I believed his story.

While leading Buster through town, I decided it was not the best thing to lead him through the main streets, so I took to side streets and alleys. You see there were plenty of horses in town on the main street and they were all frightened of wild animals and few that I had already met nearly ran away. I finally got Buster over to the country road which went near the Park and had not gone far when we met a team of young horses and I cannot yet figure how they turned around so quick and started the other way. I saw right away that this would not do for us to keep on a main road, so I started out across vacant property and at last we arrived at the Park okay. There were about thirty or forty people following us, mostly boys.

My father was surprised to see us come into the yard and me leading Buster and I was so excited about having Buster I had forgotten to tell my father that the bear had not cost me a penny, until we were eating supper, when I then handed him back his check which he had given me to help pay on the express charges.

"Well son, now that you have your bear, what do you intend doing with him?"

"I intend to put him in training but he already knows quite a few tricks and maybe someday I will put him in a show."

Buster was not a small bear at this time, he weighed about four hundred pounds. He had gained about one hundred pounds since I had last seen him. After I finished my supper, as it was called in those days in Oklahoma, I went out to play with Buster but I did not handle him very much as he was not very clean after coming on this long trip and I knew that I would have to give him a good bath in the morning. I got him to do a few of his tricks, which I had taught him while in Dyerville, California. He had not forgotten them and my father thought this was wonderful, that Buster should remember me and also to do his tricks for me as he did.

It was now getting pretty late and as I had a big day before me, I decided it was time for me to get to bed so I could be up early the next morning and start out by giving Buster his bath. I did not sleep much that night as Buster was on my mind, I was like a boy with a new toy, I could hardly wait until morning to come. I was also afraid he might get loose so I got up several times during the night to see that he was all right. Maybe I was a big daffy about Buster but if anything should happen to him now that I had him back with me, it would be a calamity.

I was up bright and early next morning and out to see that Buster got something to eat for his breakfast but he did not seem very hungry as I think he had too many peaches the day before on the train. It is hard to say how many pounds he had eaten as the expressman had kept feeding him.

The day before when I brought Buster home, I tied him to a locust tree on the south side of the house and on the opposite side of the house was the barn where we kept several head of horses and I knew that I must keep Buster at some distance from the horses until I had them used to his wild smell. I thought it would be best to take one horse at a time and lead him a little closer each day and by so doing they would become used to him. One of the horses was much more frightened than the others and it took me at least three weeks to get him within seventy five feet of Buster but there is something very remarkable about this horse, in about two months, he would go up and smell Buster. While training him to come closer, I never whipped him or abused him in any way and when he found out that Buster would not hurt him, they became good pals and I will tell you more about this horse and Buster later on in this story. The rest of the horses and mules still kept their distance of about thirty or forty feet, but would not run away when they saw him and in the course of a few months they paid no attention to him.

My father had built a large roller skating rink in the Park so it was here that Buster and I spent many hours in the morning, putting him through his tricks. I then began to teach him how to roller skate and this was the most difficult undertaking I had ever tried. The worst thing was, to keep the skates on Buster. After I would put them on him tight with large leather straps, I would block the skates by putting a small block of wood in front of the wheels, also one back of the back wheels and this would keep the skates from rolling out from under him and by coaxing him with candy, to stand up on the skates. Then as soon as he would get up and get his balance, I would push the little block of wood out from in front of the wheels and start him rolling and I would go along beside him holding one of his front paws so as to help balance him and sometimes he would go as far as seventy-five feet and then again he would only go ten feet until the skates would roll out from under him. They would generally go forward in the same way that they do when a person is learning to skate, and maybe you didn't think he came down hard on this maple floor. Sometimes I could make him go through this for four or five times, but if I laughed when he fell, he seemed to realize it and would take his front paws and tear the skates off by pieces. If I hurried I might save one skate, but he certainly ruined several pair of them. After spending several months trying to get him to take strokes on these skates, I gave it up as a failure.

Another trick I taught him was to stand on one of his front paws for at least ten or twenty seconds and I was successful in getting him to do this almost perfectly. He also did rolling summersaults, sometimes five or six of them.

While training him, I received word that there was a good bear trainer in Topeka, Kansas so I wrote him several letters in regards to the training of bears, asking plenty of questions. He wrote that he had never had any experience in training grizzly bears but that he trained at least a dozen black and brown bears. To my recollection this trainer was an Italian, anyway, he was a foreigner and I made him a proposition to come down for a month or so and help me with training Buster. He accepted the proposition and in a week or so I met him at the train and had no trouble picking him out from the few passengers who got off the train.

I took him directly to the Park where I kept Buster and of course he was very anxious to see Buster and get acquainted with him. He said that he was very fond of wild animals and especially bears. So after he had made up with Buster, I told him the story of how I had captured Buster and how I had killed his mother and sister. He thought this was very wonderful and interesting. At this time Buster weighed about five or six hundred pounds and he thought that he was an exceptionally large bear then but I explained to him that he was only about half grown and no doubt that he would reach a weight of a thousand pounds or even more and he could hardly believe it as he said that all the bears he had anything to do with didn't weight over four hundred pounds. One thing he did not like about Buster was his long claws but I explained that I had already clipped them off over half an inch.

I did not attempt to put Buster through any of his tricks the day the trainer arrived but decided to start in the next morning, so we were both up early the next morning and ready to start Buster on his training. I put Buster through the tricks which I had taught him and the trainer thought that the one where he stood on his front paw, was a very good one. I told him how I had spent so much time in trying to teach him to skate and that was one trick I certainly would like to have Buster accomplish so he suggested that we take him to the skating rink and give him another try at it. He said we might try a pair of skates on his front paws as well as his hind feet and maybe in that way he might be able to balance himself better, so I picked out the best and strongest skates, which we had there at the rink and all the leather straps I could find in the barn, also taking some off the harnesses. With all of these straps we finally got all four skates on him and ready for the try out. Buster and ourselves were within a few feet of the entrance to the skating rink, there being four or five steps leading up to the building from the outside, so when Buster got up on all four feet he started to roll toward the door, I tried my best to steer him away from the door but failed and down the steps he went on his head, rolling and tumbling. Naturally we had to laugh for it was a funny sight but Buster didn't think so, for as soon as he got to the bottom he seemed to realize that those skates were the cause of this tumble so believe me, it wasn't long until two good pair of skates were wrecked. I tried to stop him from tearing them all to pieces with his mouth, but he was bawling and making a lot of noise. The trainer stood some distance away, telling me what to do but he did not help me any. He said that I should make Buster keep those skates on but it was out of the question and was but a few minutes until he had them off. After Buster had gotten the skates off his front feet, the trainer came over to give me some assistance but Buster knew he was a stranger and figured that he had no right to be there and made a lunge for him, knocking him down and biting him on the shoulder and there is no doubt that if he had not had the skates still on his hind feet, he would have hurt him badly or might have killed him. As Buster hit him, he fell to the ground and I had hold of Busters collar doing my best to hold him back and all the time I was doing this I was telling the trainer to get up and run. It seemed a long time until he got to his feet but when he did he certainly made fast tracks. I then got Buster cooled down and got the skates off and I believe this was the angriest I had ever seen Buster.

After I had put the chain on Buster and tied him up, I went over to the trainer and asked if he was badly hurt and he said "No, I do not think I am hurt but I was never so frightened in my life." He took his shirt off and there we found quite a bruised place on his shoulder, but the skin was not torn.

I then asked him what he thought about Buster, if he thought he could be taught to skate. He said that there was no doubt but that he could be taught but he did not want the job of doing it. He also said he had no experience in training grizzly bears and as he had not been with Buster while he was a cub, he thought it would be best for him to give up this job. I really felt sorry for him, but at the same time, I decided it was best for him as Buster did not seem any too anxious to become acquainted with him. He was anxious to get started back to Topeka that evening but I persuaded him to stay over until the next day. So in the afternoon, I put Buster through six or seven of his tricks and he said he thought I was making very good headway and that there was no doubt but that I would be the only one who could do anything with Buster. He also said if I took my time and done all the training myself, I would probably have the best trained bear in the United States.

The next day I took the trainer to the train and bought him a ticket for Topeka, Kansas also handing him five dollars. I imagine he had much experience on this deal and he thanked me several times and asked me to write him once in a while and let him know how I got along with the training of Buster. He thought Buster was the finest bear he had ever seen and he had learned that there was a great difference in training a black bear and a Silver Tip Grizzly. He advised me, never give in to him and I said, "Well you ran from him" and he said, "I would probably got going a lot sooner but he scared me so badly, I could not get up."

After wishing me luck and telling me goodbye, I told him I was surely glad he could go home to his family unhurt.

After I returned to the Park, I had a long talk with my father about Buster and what had happened the day before and he thought it would be advisable to get a heavy muzzle made for Buster as he was very powerful with his teeth, especially the way he tore those skates from his feet.

The next day I took measurements of his head and nose, so as to have the muzzle made. I went into town to see several harness shops and hardware stores, trying to find out if I could get the muzzle made here in town, but was not successful. One of the hardware merchants helped me make a drawing of the muzzle and sent this to a firm in Kansas City, Missouri, who specialized in dog collars and muzzles. I soon received a letter asking if I wanted the muzzle padded with leather and hair on the back side. I advised them that it would be all right to do that but as Buster was growing so fast, perhaps they had better make the muzzle at least an inch larger all around. I then received another letter from them saying that they were sure I must have made a mistake in the measurements as they had made several bear muzzles but never one so large. So I then took more measurements as they had advised and sent to them. I began to get a big uneasy as to what this was going to cost so I wrote them and asked but after two weeks had past and no word from them, I did not know what to think but soon received a notice that there was a package at Wells Fargo Express Company from Kansas City so I went right down to get the package and of course it was the muzzle. It was C.O.D. and billed at six dollars. This was certainly very reasonable price for the way it was built. They also advised me that if it was unsatisfactory and needed changing, to send it back and they would make it right, free of charge. I took it home and put it on Buster and it fitted very good, with the exception that it was a bit large. He did not like it but I did not keep it on him all the time, only while training him. It did not take him long to learn to put the muzzle on himself, all except fastening it. He acted like a prize fighter putting on a pair of gloves. Speaking of boxing gloves, I thought I would teach him how to box but it was pretty risky as he did not realize how hard he hit and I figured that if I should happen to punch him in the eye or make him mad, I would be the one who would be knocked out or maybe squeezed to death, so I soon gave this trick up.

My next adventure with Buster, was to teach him to wrestle, this was very simple, really the easiest thing I had ever taught him and the way I went about it was, I would get him to raise up on his hind feet, then I would rub him or scratch him on the neck, which he enjoyed. I would then push him around as though I was going to push him down and he thought I was playing with him. I finally got him so that all I had to do was snap my fingers and say, "Stand up Buster" and he would always do this without hesitation. It was not hard for me to throw Buster if I wanted to, for all I had to do was to catch him under the collar and twist his hide and say, "Down Buster," and he would just fall over.

Another cunning trick I taught him was, to hold me up on his front paws just as a mother would a baby. One day I was doing this and something must have happened to attract his attention or else he became frightened for he just dropped me like a brick bat. I boxed him good two or three times in the face for this but he paid no attention to it and I guess he thought it was a good joke on me.

The next stunt I mapped out to teach him was very dangerous which was to make him open his mouth and let me put my head in it and when my father heard about it, he thought I was going just a little too far but I had all the confidence in the world that Buster would not hurt me, so I started out by opening his mouth with my hands and looking down into it and every time managed to get my head a little closer and it was but a few weeks until all I would have to say was, "Buster open your mouth wider, wider," and each time I said wider, he would obey me and I would then put about one fifth of my head in his mouth. This was one of the tricks that many of the people did not like to see me perform, saying that I was crazy. I received plenty of scoldings from my father but I knew it was a good trick, so I kept right on with it.

There was a good sized lake in the park and plenty of fish and bullfrogs in it. I would often take Buster down to the lake to give him a bath and he would try to catch the frogs. He could always find the frogs but if they were sitting on the bank in the mud, he would make a jump at them with his front paws and bury them down in the mud for a foot, so he was not very successful in catching the frogs to eat.

One day I had him on the dam of the lake which was heavily planted with willow trees, he had been jumping at the frogs and playing along the bank when all at once he turned back, began to bawl and rushed by me as though I was not there. I called to him but he paid no attention, just kept right on going. I could not figure out what had happened, so I walked down through the willows, close to the waters edge and located a Water Moccasin snake, about five feet long. I went back to the boat house and got an oar and hurried back to kill the snake. Buster had run all the way to the pavillion which was about three hundred feet away so I hurried back and took him to where his chain was and chained him up.

I then went back and got the snake, holding it on the oar but when I got within thirty or forty feet of Buster he began to bawl and growl and made several attempts to break the chain. This was the only living thing I had ever seen him afraid of, it surely did frighten him and he was very nervous and excited for a couple of days. He kept walking back and forth in a half circle and this taught me a lesson not to frighten him again. It must be one of the bear instincts, that the snake is poisonous, so keep out of their way. One thing for sure was that I was never able to get Buster back to the same place where he had seen the snake. He would come within fifty or sixty feet and sit down. It took him almost a year to forget about it.

On Sunday there was always a large crowd of people visiting the park as this was the only park near town and they came out to go boating, bathing and roller skating. One Sunday afternoon I planned to have some fun as there was about thirty or forty people in the lake bathing and I figured I would take Buster out in one of the boats for a ride and everyone seemed to get a great kick out of it. I had no trouble getting Buster into the boat as he enjoyed riding but it was hard to row as he was so heavy and I knew it would not take much to turn the boat over and sink. Of course the sightseers, boaters and bathers did not know that I intended turning the boat over while Buster was in it so after I rowed about one hundred feet from the boat house, using my judgment by not getting close to any of the bathers for they would be frightened and might drown. So after getting out a good distance, I began to tip the boat to one side and make it take water and I think Buster knew what was going to happen by the look he gave me, as much as to say, that he would stand it if I could. It was not long before the boat was taking water rapidly and as I stood up in the boat and called to all the bathers to get out of the water as my boat was sinking. The boat went down rather slow but as the water came in Buster stood up on his hind feet and we both went down with the boat. The water was about four feet deep so Buster just stood there splashing the water around with his front paws having the time of his life. There was not a bather left in the lake and even those in the row boats had pulled to shore and some of them had even locked themselves in the bath house. I had several persons tell me afterwards, that it was a scream to see everyone beat it. I had a small leash fastened to Buster and was trying to hold on to this but Buster was making his way toward the boat house but finally the water got so deep that he had to swim and I will say he was a wonderful swimmer. All this time I had managed to keep hold of the chain, finally I crawled upon Busters back and then there was so much screaming and hollering that it excited Buster so he turned right around and started for the other side of the lake, which was quite some distance. I was still on his back and stuck there until he got across the lake where he could wade out. I had a hard time getting him out of the water as he enjoyed it so much but by coaxing him I finally got him back to his cage.

Everyone seemed to enjoy this exhibition, so I got up and made an announcement that I would put on a real exhibition and the admission would be twenty five cents for adults and fifteen cents for children.

We had installed two telegraph poles on one side of the lake, about fifteen feet apart where the water was about fifteen feet deep and had hung a rope between the poles making a swing and built an incline back of the rope so that bathers could go back on this incline and get a good start and swing high in the air out over the water and then drop into the deep water. How the boys did enjoy this swing and I told the crowd my intention was to train Buster to hang onto the ring which was on this rope and swing out over the lake and turn loose. I explained that I had never tried to get him to do this stunt but I would do my best to make him do it and I also told them that I would put him through all of his tricks which he had already learned. In other words, I would be giving them the best bear show they had ever seen.

On the following day, I had a couple newspaper reporters call on me, wanting to advertise this exhibition I was going to give but I explained to them that I did not want to advertise as I was not sure how successful the show would be. I was very well acquainted with one of the reporters and he said I need not worry about how much it would cost as all they really wanted was some passes to the show and to the skating rink. This suited me fine, so I gave them twenty passes to the park, boating, skating rink and bathing. Maybe you think I didn't get advertisement, but I did. There were several towns around Hobart which had newspapers and I called on the editors and they were all very accommodating and advertised for a few passes. They advertised just what stunts I was putting Buster through and sent copies of the papers to me.

I was plenty busy getting ready for this exhibition which I had promised to the public. This was my first show I had with Buster and I had promised I would try to get him to swing out over the lake and drop into the water, so I had to get busy training him.

When the two reporters were there at the park, I had explained to them that I would have to begin training immediately so as to do this new stunt and they remarked that they would like to see me give him his first try out. I told them that it would be okay but that they would have to stay back a considerable distance for I had found out that when teaching him new stunts, it was much better if we two were alone. Strangers often drew his attention away from what I was teaching him. So I told them I would let them know when I started training.

When I got ready for training I let the reporters know and they were right there when I took Buster down to the swinging rope but as the triangle which was on the rope was almost two feet too low for Buster, I had to tie it up higher and I got it so high that I was unable to reach it myself, so I had one of the reporters go to the pavilion and bring me a soda pop case on which I could stand and hold the triangle. The first thing was to show Buster just what the triangle was for, so I held onto the triangle and would swing out over the water a few feet and must have done this about ten times and it wasn't long until Buster was putting out his paws trying to catch hold of the triangle. In a short time, I had him holding onto it but he would not hold himself up. He would walk to the edge of the water and then walk back with the triangle. I must have kept this up for two or three hours, so about as far as I got this day was, that he held on to the triangle and would walk to the water and back. The reporters seemed to get quite a kick out of watching and said that I had more patience than any fellow they ever heard tell about. Naturally a reporter can ask questions faster and more of them than any five persons and when they left for town they asked if they might come back the next day or so and watch the training again but I told them I thought it would be best for them to wait until the following Saturday and no doubt that by that time he would have accomplished the stunt for I intended to work him every day.

Buster seemed in the best mood for months, never getting cross, nervous or excited as you know wild animals get very restless at times, so I had all this in my favor. I usually put Buster through his training in the morning as there was always quite a crowd of people in the park in the afternoon, boating and bathing.

Every few days my father would say, "Sonny, I think you are just wasting a lot of time and going to a lot of trouble in training that bear and you do not know when he will turn on you, perhaps striking you or squeezing you to death." I told him I got a big kick out of it and was sure that someday it would bring me good returns. He said, "If you know how much I worry about you, I am sure you would get rid of him or at least putting him through those stunts." Of course there were times that Buster would get angry and bawl and strike the ground with his paws but never seemed to frighten me as I would just go right up to him and pet him and talk to him.

While training him, you would be surprised to know that at some times, I would feed him as much as two pounds of candy a day. There was one special kind which was his favorite and that was a mixed cream candy. We had a small confectionary store in the skating rink, so you see I got the candy wholesale. I always had candy in my pockets but Buster did not get all of it as I was getting the habit also.

The next morning, I was up real early so as to get Buster out on the rope, trying to make him swing out over the lake. He was always so glad to see me come to where he was chained, regardless of the time, eight times out of ten he would stand up on his hind feet, licking his chops and I figured that this was his way of greeting me. This day I planned a new way to get him to swing on the rope as I tied the triangle still higher on the rope so he would have to get up on the box to reach it, thinking that when he got his paws through the triangle, I would take a small stick and hit the toes of his hind feet, making him lift them up and when he got his weight off the box, I would pull it out from under him and then he would naturally begin to swing. This worked very nice until he swung a few feet and let loose. I continued to make him go over this again and again until it must have been at least seventy five times and I was absolutely all in and Buster was getting tired and disgusted. I remember how he used to look at me with his one eye and I could almost read his thoughts, that I was just making a clown out of him. In the afternoon I would put him through all of his other tricks so he would be in good training and our show would be a success.

It was soon advertised all over town that I was putting Buster through all of his training also through the task of swinging on the rope and the public began to come out from town around nine o'clock to watch me so I finally had to lock the gates to the park letting no one in until after twelve o'clock.

The reporters came out Friday night to see if it was okay for them to come out next morning to take some pictures. I gave my consent but warned them that they were to bring no friends with them. So Saturday morning, I started Buster out on his stunt of swinging over the lake and had him doing it so good that he would hang onto the triangle and go out over the lake at least thirty feet. He seemed to realize he was up in the air and was not taking any chances of dropping into the water. The reporters thought that was great and they gave me a great deal of praise. I told them that the hardest thing to do was, to get Buster to turn loose of the triangle when he was out over the lake but seemed to enjoy swinging on the rope and would hang on as long as the rope would swing. It was even hard to make him turn loose of the triangle as he had so much fun with it.

I thought of making a trick hinge in the triangle and tie a small rope to it and when Buster was out over the water, I would pull this rope and the triangle would come in two in the middle and this would let Buster drop in the water, but I knew if I played this trick on him, I would have a hard time getting him to even swing on the rope, so I gave up this idea.

One day I got a ladder and climbed up onto the rope and when Buster swung out, I swung with him, figuring that when he got out over the water, I would slap him in the face or step on his paws and thus make him turn loose but this did not work for when I put all my weight on his paws, he did not even pay any attention to it, I even went so far as to kick him in the head and then I got to thinking he might grab my foot and pull me in with him and my father mentioned that the rope might break letting us both go down but I told him I was not afraid if it did happen but if it did happen on Sunday, it would make a good stunt. He talked me out of it though and no doubt if he had not, I would have had someone cut the rope.

I had about lost my patience in trying to get Buster to do what I wanted him to do, so decided I would have to let it go at that.

Now as we had several acres of watermelons close to the park, my father suggested that he would give the public all the nice cold melons they could eat and this was also put in the advertisement in local papers. So the Saturday before the big show, we hauled in two wagon loads of melons to the ice plant in town. There were about one hundred twenty five melons to a wagon load and each melon averaged about twenty five pounds. Oklahoma was noted for raising large watermelons and our plan was to haul these melons back to the park Sunday about eleven o'clock, so they would be good and cold and the public would certainly enjoy them.

Speaking of watermelons, you would probably be surprised to know that Buster could go out in the field and pick out a ripe melon as he never failed but he would damage the vines as he would pull the melons and vines all up and how he did like a good ripe melon. I would let him hunt a ripe one and then I could cut it off for him and make him carry it out to the edge of the patch before eating it. Now this was his style of eating a melon, he would take the melon in his front paws and squeeze it until it burst open then he would pick out all the seeds and eat them, then eat the rind, always leaving the heart until the last. You see he did not do as people do, for most of them eat the heart first. If Buster ate too many melons, they would make him sick so I figured two melons were a good feast for him.

We spent two or three days getting the park all decorated with flags and bunting, hauling in chairs and tables for the people to use for their lunch and also the watermelon. We figured that there would be around a thousand or fifteen hundred so we were anxious to have the park looking at its best and wanting everyone to have a good time.

Always on Saturday night the skating rink was kept open until twelve or one o'clock, so the Saturday night before the show, I turned in early, letting some of the help take care of closing the rink, as I had gone through a strenuous week, so thought it best to get a nights rest so I would be all set for the big day.

Sunday morning I was up about six thirty and on looking out of the window, what do you think I saw. There out in the front of the gates were spring people in spring wagons and surreys. I called my father and told him, "Just look outside, there are some folks who intend to put in a good day and not miss any of the show." And my father said, "Are you sure you did not advertise that you gave breakfast with the show?"

I hurried down to the park gates to meet them and they wanted to know just where was the best place to put their teams. We had made arrangements to use the adjoining pasture for the parking of the teams and wagons, so I told them to follow me. I opened the gate to the pasture and told them I was sure there would be plenty of room for all as there was twenty acres in this pasture. You see everyone had to travel by horse and buggy or wagon so most of them would want to hitch their teams to the back of their vehicles as they brought feed for the animals, so you see they would take up considerable space. I told the people who had just come that we had not yet opened the park gates or started to sell tickets but if they wanted to go in, I would collect the fee for the tickets. I asked them how far they had come and they said that they were from Roosevelt, Oklahoma, which was some twenty miles from Hobart. I had no more than finished collecting from them and showed them the entrance to the park, when looking down the road, I saw two more outfits coming.

I hurried into the house and grabbed a bit of breakfast and finished dressing for the occasion and by the time I had finished it was nearly eight o'clock and there were at least eight or ten buggies, surries and wagons waiting to be taken care of and enter the park. We had made arrangements for extra help for the day, but as yet they had not arrived, so father and I were busy men but by eleven o'clock everything was working perfectly and there was about a thousand people in the park and still coming and by one o'clock there was over thirty five hundred people that had passed through the gates and I began to wonder if the twenty acre pasture was going to hold all the different kinds of vehicles, from two wheeled carts, buggies, surries, wagons, saddle horses and bicycles.

No doubt but that there were many people who had entered without paying admission but this did not worry me for I was really surprised that there were so many who had already paid and I figured that we had made quite a clean up.

Nearly in the center of the park we had built a platform on which the band sat and this platform was about twenty feet square and three feet high and this is where I was to have Buster do most of his stunts.

Buster had been very much advertised in Kiowa County so that the people of the county as well as all the small towns of other counties were anxious to see Buster and his tricks. Everyone was so anxious for the show to start but we had planned the starting time about three o'clock as this would give all a chance to go boating, bathing and skating and also eat their lunch and watermelon before the show started. To my recollection there was about half enough melon for all these people but all seemed to enjoy themselves.

We had engaged a speaker, and if I remember right his name was Mr. Allen and also the Hobart City Band was to do the honor of furnishing the music.

Mr. Allen's first announcement was, that Mr. Briles and his son were very much surprised and glad to see so many people come to the park to see the show, which they were sure everyone would enjoy. Mr. Allen kept the platform for about twenty minutes telling of the development of this park as this was the only amusement park anywhere around in this new country. One thing I remember in particular was that he cautioned all who ate melon, to be sure to put all rinds in the garbage containers for if they did not, they would draw the flies.

The band amused the crowd for several hours and also played for the people who were roller skating.

Oh yes, there is one thing I forgot to mention, there were about three or four hundred Indians in the crowd and you would see the majority sitting on the ground watching the different amusements.

I had built a pen about thirty feet square and six feet high and in the center of this I had chained Buster so no one could reach him to tease him, also he would not be able to climb the fence. Around this pen, you would see most of the Indians, all passing their opinion about Buster. There seemed to be many arguments between them.

I began to get very uneasy as the time drew near for the show as there had been so much noise and so many people around that I was sure Buster was feeling the effects of all this excitement so I was getting anxious to get it over with.

Before the show was to start, we moved all the chairs from the band stand and we had arranged it so the rails could be removed from the sides of the platform, it took but a few minutes to get ready but we wanted it so that everyone could see the performance.

Mr. Allen made another short speech, telling them where Buster the Silver Tip Grizzly was captured and how he was captured, who had trained him and warned all to keep as quiet as possible and not stand on the tables for he hoped that everyone would get a chance to see everything.

While Mr. Allen was speaking, I had taken Buster out of his pen and around back of the pavillion so that when Mr. Allen called me, I would be ready for him. Very few people had seen me do this and when Mr. Allen had finished his speech, he stepped to the rear of the band stand and called to me, that it was all right for me to come on the stand but please give him a few seconds to get off the stand.

As Buster and I mounted the steps, he seemed to be in the best of humor, but just the same I was a bit nervous and excited. I explained to the people that Buster was just as tame as any ordinary dog and picking up one of his front paws, I showed the people that his claws were much longer than any dogs and also that I had clipped off a part of each claw. I then explained what he could do if he so chose or if he really got mad, how with just one hit or so with those paws, or if he ever got you in his arms and squeezed you, well it would be a quick death. But as long as he was treated with kindness, no jokes or tricks played on him, it was all right.

"The first thing I want to do is to prove that he is harmless and will not hurt me." Then removing the muzzle form his head, I took Busters mouth between my hands and opened it very wide, putting my hand into it and catching hold of his tongue and the next thing was to get him to open his mouth of his own accord by my just talking to him. I usually had to speak very snappy several times to make him open it very wide and whenever I thought he had it opened as wide as he could get it, I would get my head close to his mouth. There was a great deal of disturbance among the people as I did this and some of the women screamed and after this stunt I received a great applause.

I then made Buster raise up on his hind feet, handing him his muzzle which he put on himself with the exception of fastening the straps and here Buster got all the cheers. As there was so much noise of whistling and clapping of hands, I began to get uneasy that Buster might make an attempt to leave the stand and go back to his pen where he had been chained, so I asked them to please keep a little more quiet. Of course this was hard for them to do for the majority of these people had never seen a trained bear.

While Buster was standing there, I made him put his paws on my shoulders and then put his arms all the way around me and by this time I handed Buster a piece of candy, telling the crowd that he was a great deal like a child, he would do anything for a piece of candy, but Buster never seemed to get enough candy.

I had arranged a set of steps on which I had Buster climb up four steps on his front paws and then back down. The first time I put him through this trick he went down the four steps all okay but when he got to the top he sat down looking at the crowd and they all began to cheer and clap their hands but I explained that this was not all of the stunt, that he was supposed to walk up and then down without letting himself down and if all would keep quiet, I would make him do it. So I took him to the back of the steps and finally got him started up and by talking rather sharply to him, he did the trick perfectly. It was rather hard to get him to do the same trick the second time as I had trained him when he had done it once, he could then walk over the steps on his hind feet, but he acted very well.

I then brought him up to the front of the stand and made him stand on one front paw for at least ten seconds and I do not believe there is any bear trained to do this trick for that length of time. Buster then lifted me up on his two front arms as high as he could and next he laid down and played dead. I could always get him to lie down okay but was hard to get him to lay his head out flat but he did very well. He then got on his four feet and I got on his back riding him around the stand a couple times and this was about all the show on the platform, so I went to the rear and asked Mr. Allen to please come up on the platform and explain to the crowd just what the next event would be so he explained to them that the next stunt on the stand was to wrestle the bear and that anyone who would come up and wrestle the bear and throw him, there was twenty dollars prize money. He then went on to mention that at four thirty sharp, Buster would swing out over the lake but he also explained that I had not had enough time to train Buster to turn loose of the triangle and drop into the water.

I then came forward and invited anyone in the crowd to come up and wrestle with Buster, also told them that I would guarantee that Buster would not hurt them. I waited some three or four minutes but no one seemed to want to take the chance. One fellow spoke up, "You know you would be safe in making that prize one hundred dollars instead of twenty." I then told them that I was going to show them how easy it was to throw a bear weighing seven hundred pounds. I grabbed hold of Buster and began to tussle with him, both of us almost falling off the platform. This of course looked very real to the public but in reality, it was only play but sometimes his claws would go rather deep into my back and hurt so I would have to scold him and box him, we must have kept this up for at least three or four minutes and everyone got a great kick out of it. I finally got hold of Buster under his collar and as I had a corn husker on my hand, I gave him a good hard pinch and he just fell over. I really believe that the majority of the people thought that I threw him by my own strength. I would be safe in saying that twenty fellows like myself would not be able to throw him.

After the wrestling match was over, I advised everyone how to get over to where the swing on which Buster was to do his next stunt but most of them wanted to see more of Buster on the stand. The Indians especially stayed until the last or until I took Buster away.

We had about twenty boats on the lake and everyone was occupied with from four to six people in each boat as they could get in a good location to see this next stunt. Most of the people had to stay on the opposite side of the lake across from the swing, which was about two hundred and fifty feet distance. The rest stood near the boat house which was at one side of the swing. It was a bit difficult for many to get close to the swing as it was on the dam which was at the back and about forty or fifty feet high.

Everyone had plenty of time to get their places before I brought Buster out on the dam, he seemed to be enjoying all this notoriety and certainly in the best of humor. After Buster and I arrived at the swing, I advised all bathers and people in the boats to keep close to the bank of the lake as Buster might take a notion to drop off into the water and as the water was about twenty feet deep at this place, he might, after coming up, start for the first boat, turning it over and drowning someone. Now the band had taken their chairs and placed them on the boat landing and just as they started to play The Star Spangled Banner, I had Buster take hold of the triangle, getting back as far as he could, so as to get a good swing when he started out. He must have gone twenty five or thirty feet in the air and he certainly got a kick out of this and the second time he went out, he raised his hind feet up to the triangle, trying to get his feet into it. I had not trained him to do this but he seemed to know that there was a crowd looking at him and he was trying to be a clown. Now let me tell you, this was a great stunt and very exciting to see, the only thing I regretted was, that I could not make him turn loose of the triangle for some time. After this I took him back to his pen and here I took off his muzzle. He was so glad to get this off and from then on everyone was feeding him candy and peanuts and I am sure that this was the biggest feed of sweets he had ever had and believe me he was fed several hundred sacks of peanuts and was a big wonder that he was not sick but he seemed to survive all right.

The crowd stayed until quite late that night and after all had gone and we had paid the band and the extra helpers, we had taken in several hundred dollars from the gate fees, and concessions of boating, bathing, and skating. So the next morning I told my father that the park stock had advanced and I also told him, "Do you remember the day I came to you and asked you for the money to help pay the express on Buster and at that time you said, what good is a bear and what can you do with him, so now I think that the bear stock has also gone up." He had to own up that I had put on a wonderful exhibit but he said that there was one thing he did not like and that was putting my head in Buster's mouth and that I must stop it. He said that when he saw me do this, the cold chills ran up and down his back.

For the rest of the summer we gave a show with Buster about every two weeks, which always seemed to draw the crowd. We did not charge an entrance fee as all we wanted was to have the crowd come out and rent the boats, go bathing and roller skating.

Our plans were to close the park the latter park of September and go into town for the winter as there was not much doing at the park during the winter months.

We had a Feed Mill in town, also handling coal and wood and were out on the edge of the business section of town and as we had quite a large piece of property on which the mill and coal sheds were built, so on the rear of this property I built a pen about twenty five feet square. This went underground on a slant for about ten feet and was lined with granite rock so that he would not be able to dig out. I built this as I had been advised that Buster should have a cave in which to go during the winter months while hibernating.

One day I happened to leave the chain off of Buster and I guess when he discovered that he was loose, he went over the top of the high picket fence. It must have been about noon for he went to the public school and the children were just coming out for lunch hour. Some of the children were afraid and ran from him but there were three or four boys who had fed him candy and nuts in his pen and knew him pretty well. So, one of them ran to the nearest store and bought a nickel's worth of candy and by this time enticed Buster to follow him into the school grounds and down into the school basement.

It was not long until they found me and told me that Buster was at the school. I could scarcely believe this until I had gone to the pen and discovered that he was really gone and I certainly did make tracks to the school and as my father had warned me that Buster was going to hurt some person or child and then we would be sued for damages. This kept running through my mind all the time I was running to the school which was about three blocks away. Upon arriving at the school, I found the children and the professor, who was keeping the children all well back from Buster, feeding him candy. He said that it was the only thing he knew to do, for as long as he had candy, he would sit down and seemed perfectly satisfied. As Buster did not have his muzzle on I told the professor that I was very uneasy but the professor said that it had been a great treat to the children. He also mentioned that he had been at the show the day I gave the exhibition and he thought that he was the best and largest trained bear he had ever seen in his life. I told him that Buster had at least another year to grow. One or two of the teachers who were standing near asked me if I could make him do some of his tricks as some of the children had never seen him perform. I told them that I would try but that he had been fed so much candy, I was a bit doubtful as to whether I could get him to do any, nevertheless I would try. He managed to do a few, thus giving the children quite a show.

Now as Buster had neither muzzle or chain on him, I just caught hold of his collar and lead him out of the basement and after getting him outside, he followed me back to the cage, just like a dog. Several hundred of the school children followed to the end of the school grounds and no doubt would have followed all the way to the cage, had their teachers let them. The store keeper who had a little store close to the school, called out and said that he had certainly done a great candy business that day.

I had received letters from different shows, fairs and carnivals in regard to Buster. They wanted to date me up for the coming season as news of the exhibition I had given had spread all over Oklahoma and I was told that a certain newspaper in Kansas City had given me a write-up and things began to look pretty good for the next season.

Right here I want to tell you of an instance which happened, it might sound funny but it was not funny at the time. One day someone had taken a tomato can which had the top out of it and they put some sorghum molasses in it, putting it inside of Buster's cage where he could reach it after they had fed him all they could on a stick which they dipped into the molasses and let Buster lick it off the stick. He managed to get this can and in trying to get the rest of the molasses out of the can, he got his paw fastened in the can and must have had it on for some time and tried to get it off and when he could not, he began to hit his paw on the ground, thinking that by doing so he could get it off. Well, he got the can fastened on so tight that his paw began to swell and he began to bawl and make an awful noise. Someone notified me that there was something wrong with Buster so I got there as fast as I could and that is what I found. Now I knew that it was a very ticklish job to get that can off his paw as it was so badly swollen that the upper part of his paw had dropped down over the top of the can at least an inch or more. Now the question was, how to get this off as he was very angry and it was dangerous to fool with him for if I made one bad move he could kill me. I went for help and brought my father and two other men, whom I knew very well and we talked it over just what was the best thing to do. As there was a large telephone pole on one side of his cage, I thought that if we could get him over near there, I might get him up against it and wrap the chain around his body and the pole. After trying several times, I managed to do this and then with three other pieces of rope which we tied to each paw, we pulled them tight and fastened the ropes to the large timbers of the cage. Of course I was the only one inside the cage as the rest stayed outside but helped tie the ropes. The way Buster was cutting up and bawling made me very nervous and I scarcely knew what I was doing. I took a pair of tin snips and tried to cut it but could not get them started so I had to take a chisel and managed to get a hole started in the can so that I could get the tin snips in and start to cut it and when I got the can a little over half cut, it seemed as though it just split all the rest of the way by itself, for it must have been the pressure of the swollen paw which did this. Buster seemed to realize that I was trying to help him and after the can was removed, I untied him and he at once began to lick his paw. I petted his head and also rubbed his paw and he would lick my hand, showing how he appreciated the kindness I had done for him. He had a very sore paw for a week or ten days but finally healed up and never bothered him again.

As winter was approaching and I knew that Buster would soon be going into the cave to hibernate, I had another wild idea that I wanted to have Buster fight a large dog. I had a chum by the name of Powell and both he and I together decided that it would be great to have a fight between Buster and a dog and we could have it in the Opera House of Hobart. Of course we had to find a dog large enough, so we began to inquire all around and finally did locate one of the largest bull dogs I have ever seen in my life. This dog belonged to a farmer who lived about three miles from town. I do not remember the mans name but he explained to us that this dog had killed several steers so you can see that he was a very powerful dog. He must have weighed about eighty or ninety pounds but he was getting along in years, I would say about eight years old. We put our proposition to the farmer, that we would like to have his dog fight Buster and that we were willing to give him five dollars and ten passes to the fight, for the use of the dog. Of course I really do think that he was glad to get rid of the dog but he did not let us know it. After the final agreement was made and we started to get into the buggy, he asked when we wanted the dog and I told him that we would take him anytime so he said we might just as well take him along with us now, saving us a trip out to the farm, so we said okay.

He thought it might be best as we could make friends with the dog in the meantime but cautioned us not to let any children get near him or any other dogs for he had killed every dog he had ever had a fight with. This did not worry me much, that is, that he would hurt Buster, for I was pretty sure of him. When we got into town, we took the dog right over to Busters cage and he became very angry and barked and tried to get into the cage, but it did not seem to bother Buster.

We went ahead and made all arrangements for the fight, building a large cage on the stage out of hog wire and several days before we were to have the fight, Powell would lead the bull dog around and then I would lead Buster down the street and around the Court House Square and in this way we did our advertising. However if the dog came anywhere near Buster, it was almost impossible to hold him, but Buster was very much unconcerned. We had made signs and placed them on Buster as well as the dog. They were made of canvas and the one on the dog read, "This is the Dog who is to fight Buster the Silver Tip Grizzly Bear in the Opera House." The sign on Buster read, "This is the Bear who is to fight the Bull Dog in the Opera House."

I do not remember the dates but I think it was the latter part of October. This was a very successful advertising campaign, leading the bear and the dog around the streets every day before the fight. One day I mentioned to Powell, "Do you think that the dog would be crazy enough to tackle a bear and I have a notion to try him out somewhere." Powell suggested that we take him into a coal shed which was near and that I go get Buster and lead him into the shed putting him into the rear end of it, so that when the dog entered the door, if he wanted to get away, he could. I put Buster's muzzle on and trimmed his claws as I did not want him to hurt the dog before the fight. All we really wanted to know was, if the dog had the nerve to tackle the bear. I was feeding Buster some apples while Powell went to get the dog and by the time he brought the dog to the entrance, he was barking and growling so much that Powell could hardly hold him. He asked me if he should turn the dog loose, but he gave him enough rope to get at Buster and if Buster started to hurt him, he could get him away. I had chained Buster to the side of the coal shed and he only had about twenty five feet of slack and as Buster was still sitting on his haunches eating the apples which had been given him, paying no attention whatsoever to the dog. Finally, Powell gave the dog more rope and he ran in and started to grab Buster right around the neck and by this time I was climbing upon the wall of the shed and when I looked down, the dog was away at the other end of the shed, which was about fifteen or twenty feet. I did not see just what happened but Powell told me afterwards, as near as he could, that Buster just hit the dog one lick with his paw and sent him away to the other end of the shed. The dog was game as he got right up and was going back to tackle Buster again. Buster did not seem to pay any attention to him but I told Powell to pull the dog away and take him back to the barn where we were keeping him.

We examined the dog thoroughly to see if he was hurt in any way, but he seemed to be alright. I then put Buster back in his cage and Powell and I talked the matter over and figured that the fight was going to be a great event and that we were going to make several hundred dollars out of it.

Three days before that date of the fight, every ticket was sold, also tickets for standing room. If I remember right, the Opera House was to get forty percent of the gross receipts, so they were making good money also.

My father had been telling me that he did not want me to go ahead with this fight for he was sure that the bear would squeeze the dog to death in just a few minutes and he said that it was not right to do this. I explained to him that we were going to keep a leash on the dog and also on Buster so that if we saw the bear getting the best of the dog we could separate them. Of course, I knew that if Buster ever got hold of the dog, he would not have a chance to live three minutes.

Now the whole town was wild about this bear and dog fight and were anxious for the day to come. Early the morning of the fight, I went to the Opera House and on the door of the main entrance was tacked a notice which stated that the bear and dog fight could not be held in town as it was against the City Charter and was signed by the Mayor of Hobart. I made haste and went at once up to see the Mayor and had quite a talk with him. He told me that this fight was against my father's wishes and that he had also had about fifty complaints from other citizens who were against it, also that the town people would think much more of Powell and me. I explained to him that we had sold all of the tickets and that we had gone to a lot of expense, building the cage on the stage, having the tickets printed and advertising. I also said that I did not know if the Opera House manager would release us or not, but he told me that the only thing I could do was refund all the money to the people and call the fight off. He said, "Of course, if you are determined to have a cruel thing like this happen, you would have to make it outside of the city limits so that it will be out of my jurisdiction, also if that bear should kill the dog, no doubt but that there would be several who would prosecute me, for cruelty to animals."

Well I had to make up my mind to give up the fight and I felt pretty bad about disappointing the public, also about giving back all that money. Quite a few of the young men wanted me to go outside the city limits and still have the fight. I also had a sweetheart who advised me that if I didn't call this fight off, she was through with me, so off it was called.

The manager of the Opera House refunded the money and said that he was certainly sorry that the City had given the order to cancel the fight. We, of course, had a lot of fun and excitement getting ready for this fight and, of course, Powell and myself had seen just a little of what might have been when we had the try out in the shed.

If you remember I told you that I would tell you more about Buster and the horse. Occasionally I would take him out for a ride in the spring wagon and he seemed to get so much pleasure out of a ride but always had a habit of trying to get out on the horse's back. I could never figure out why he wanted to do this, so one day I had him out for a ride and he took a notion to get on the horse's back and usually frightened me a little as I was afraid that the horse might run away, but I got out and got hold of the bridle and tried to hold the horse and give Buster the chance to do whatever it was he wanted. He crawled out and put his front paws on the back of the horse and then got back in the wagon. I could not figure just what he wanted to do unless it was that he had seen us riding horseback and he thought he could do it. It would have been quite a stunt to have a horse for him to ride but he was too large. I do not think I could have found a horse whose back would have held him up and really believe the horse would have run away. After that when I took Buster for his rides, I would always chain him to the seat so he could only go so far.

Buster also had another odd habit, several times I caught him standing on his hind feet with his front paws held straight up over his head and he would turn around and around, sometimes keeping this up for several minutes. I never could figure out why he did this unless it was to get dizzy, and perhaps he got a kick out of it.

I have never explained in the story just what and how I fed Buster. A bear will eat most anything you give him and no doubt if he was hungry enough, he would eat an old shoe. But Buster from the day I brought him home had plenty of food and good food too. The largest hotel in town, which was called the Central Hotel, always saved a bushel basket full of good pieces of bread, meat and scraps from the tables. They never charged me anything for this as my father and myself always boarded at the hotel during the winter months. I always handed the dishwasher fifty to seventy-five cents per week, figuring that I was getting off pretty cheap. It took as much to feed him as it would to feed four or five hogs. Once in a while the produce house would call me and tell me that they had a barrel of rotten apples or some other kind of fruit which was spoiling, and for me to come and get it and give it to Buster. I was always glad to get this as it was Buster's favorite food, spoiled fruit. Here is a queer thing, I took Buster a barrel of apples, he would almost always turn the barrel over and with all the apples out on the ground, he would pick out all the rotten ones and eat them first, saving the ones which were less rotten for the last. I am pretty safe in saying that I have seen him eat seventy-five pounds of apples at a time and am sure he would have eaten more if I would give them to him. He never did get sick on apples but I do remember one instance when I fed him some pineapple, which had just started to sour, this made him very sick, and he vomited most of them up and this is the only time I ever saw him get sick while I had him.

His most favorite fruit was blackberries and raspberries, especially when they were over ripe. You have probably wondered why Buster grew so large but if you will stop to figure out what he ate every day, it is no wonder that he gained about a pound a day. Of course, he did not gain during the winter months while in hibernation.

As winter had already begun, Buster was not in his cave for a good sleep. It is seldom that a bear comes out of hibernation after once going in, or until they are through with their rest. They do not eat or take any water during this time and lose very little weight. This particular winter, to my recollection, Buster did not stay in the cave very long, not much over eight weeks. The cause might have been that the winter was so mild.

During these winter months, I was making plans to have my own road show. So early in the spring I was told by one of my friends that there were two men in town who were trying to locate the boy who owned the grizzly bear. They finally located me and told me that they had a proposition to place before me, in which they wished to use the bear to advertise one of the largest Breweries which was located in St. Louis, Missouri. They were very anxious to see Buster and wanted me to put him through some of his stunts. But I explained that he had just come out of his cave and that he did not have much pep. I told them that it would be difficult to get him to do any of his tricks but that I would do my best.

I made arrangements to meet them at the Central Hotel and there we talked over their propositions. I told them that I had planned to have my own road show but I might consider their proposition. They wanted to go down and see Buster and see what he could do before any of the details were gone into. When we got to the cage, Buster was standing on his hind legs waiting for me, as he so often did. I then unlocked the gate and opened it and invited the two men to come in with me but they had disappeared. There was a large coal shed close by and they had run to the other side of it. I called to them and told them that there was no danger as Buster was chained inside the cage. One of them called to me saying that Buster looked too large and he did not intend to get too close to that gate.

After I got inside and closed the gate, both the men came over within ten or fifteen feet of the cage. I explained to them how Buster had been captured and what kind of a bear he was. Also, I told them that I would take the large chain off him and put a small one on and bring him outside of the cage, but one of them insisted that I keep him inside and try to get him to do some of his stunts. I told them that there was not really enough room for him and that he could do so much better when I took him out where he had plenty of room.

I unlocked the gate and both men ran at least a hundred and fifty feet away and I had quite a time in convincing them that Buster was as tame as a dog and that they were safe in coming close to him. They finally managed to come closer to him and I showed them that Buster was perfectly harmless, I jumped on his back and rode him around and then put him through several stunts. They watched Buster very close for they had really expected to see a little black bear which weighed about three hundred pounds. Buster was nearly through shedding at this time and had a beautiful coat of fur. It was very dark brown, the tips being silver. The only thing he was not very clean as he had been lying in the dirt. After he had done several stunts, the two men were sure that I was just the person they were looking for. So we made arrangements to meet later at the hotel and perhaps we would come to some agreement.

I went home and dressed in my best, so I would make a good impression. I met them about seven p.m. and they had already made out the contract for Buster and myself. No doubt but that you will be surprised to know what they wanted Buster and myself to do. Perhaps you will remember that there was a beer on the market, and on its' label was the picture of a bear standing up drinking a bottle of beer. Well that is the Brewing Company which wanted Buster and myself to advertise for them. The contract which they had made out read as follows: (that is, to the best of my recollection)

Hobart, Oklahoma
May 10, 1904

"This agreement made between Mr. Bates, Agent for Brewing Company, located in St. Louis, Missouri and Frank Briles, Hobart, Oklahoma.

"Mr. Briles agrees to furnish one Silver Tip Grizzly Bear, named Buster, and himself, for the advertising of the Brewing Company. He is to go to any town or city in the United States, in which we wish to have him out on an exhibition. He will be booked several weeks ahead and will be allowed plenty of time for transportation of himself and bear. The principal engagements will be in towns and cities where they are holding fairs, carnivals or other celebrations.

"His instructions will be mailed to him. He may use his own judgment as to getting up the exhibition which will make the best showing before the public.

"We agree to pay Mr. Briles, the sum of Two Hundred ($200.00) Dollars per month and all expenses, a period of at least four months."

Signed by: _____

After all the business was finished, Mr. Bates invited me to have dinner with them and after this, we would plan our first performance. While we were at dinner, I mentioned that there was to be a carnival in Hobart in about ten days. I suggested that I give my first performance in my own home town. It would take me at least five or six days to get ready to ship Buster out of town as he would have to have a new crate built, in which to ship him for he had outgrown his old one.

Mr. Bates thought this a fine suggestion and I do not see where they could find a better place to give the first exhibition for if I remember rightly there were in the neighborhood of fifty saloons besides the gambling houses and honky-tonks.

After dinner, we went in to the hotel lobby, talking over the best arrangements for the program. Mr. Bates said, "Well it is at least settled that the first performance will be here in Hobart and I think that Mr. Briles can give us some suggestions as to what would be best for this town."

I told them that there would be a parade with decorated floats, carriages, buggies and wagons and there is no doubt but that we can make arrangements to put a float in the parade. This they thought was a good idea.

The gentleman with Mr. Bates, suggested that we take a wagon and have a large frame built on it, something like a hay rack, and have this all caged in with heavy hog wire, so that there would be no danger of the bear breaking loose and hurting someone. Mr. Bates did not like this idea of the wire cage as he said it would not be much of an advertisement as he intended to pass beer out to the public as the float passed by. It would also be hard to put Buster through his stunts all caged up.

Mr. Bates asked me if I thought Buster would sit in a large arm chair which would be pushed up close to a table, give him a bottle of beer to hold between his paws and drink. I told him it would be fine but that we would not give Buster the beers as it would intoxicate him but that I would fix about fifteen bottles of sweetened water and he would enjoy it and would be easy to handle.

Now Mr. Bates plans were to get a very large round table, seating four or five men around it besides Buster. They were to be playing cards and each having a bottle of beer in front of him and Buster drinking his sweetened water. He then said he thought it would be a good advertisement to have four young men on the float, passing out ice cold beer. The young men were to pull the caps and hand them to the public. He would like to have room for at least twenty cases of beer on the float and that would not last long where there were twelve or fifteen thousand people expecting to get a least one bottle of beer. One of the men suggested that they take one or two of their large beer wagons, in which they delivered the beer, putting about seventy five or a hundred cases on each wagon and place them about two blocks apart on the side of the street and when the float came along, just exchange the empties for full cases. By doing this they would be able to pass out at least two hundred cases of beer, each case containing three dozen pint bottles. This would be approximately seven thousand bottles.

Now the next step suggested was, that after the parade, I was to take Buster leading him by his chain, and call on all the saloons, which handled their brand of beer. And in the meantime, I was to put Buster through some of his tricks in each saloon, but must be different ones in each saloon and every one in the saloon was to be treated to a pint bottle of beer, no charge. I surely laughed at this for I told them that the whole town would be intoxicated in no time. I realized the fact that they did not care how much it cost, so long as they got good advertisement of their product.

It was now getting pretty late and Mr. Bates said that he would meet me the next morning about nine o'clock and go down to the distributing house and tell them our plans and perhaps they might have some other suggestions to make.

That night after I arrived home, all that I could think of was the Two hundred Dollars per month I was to receive, also all expenses. I wondered if Mr. Bates had once given a thought as to how much Buster and I would eat. Well, he made the bargain, so guess I had no worries coming.

At this time I was working in a feed elevator which was paying me seventy five dollars per month but of course I had all my expenses to pay out of that. You see I figured that I would be just about the highest paid man in Hobart.

The next morning I was up bright and early ad I had to go down and see Buster and love him, just as an old maid loves a cat. You do not know how much I loved him but you know how a person gets attached to a dog or cat, but few seldom to a Silver Tip Grizzly Bear, so therefore, I figured he was quite the most wonderful of pets.

As I had agreed to meet the advertising agents at the distributing house of their company, I was there on time. Mr. Brooks was the manager of the distributing house, with whom I was very well acquainted. I explained to him that I was there to meet Mr. Bates and the other gentleman, who were from Oklahoma City, Oklahoma, in regards to using myself and Buster as advertisement for their beer.

Now Mr. Brooks had seen me put Buster through his tricks at least a dozen times, he explained to me that he had written to the main office of advertising in Oklahoma City and suggested the idea of getting Buster and myself to do some advertising for them. I thanked him for this as it surely meant a lot to me.

Mr. Bates and his friend arrived and we started in on making plans for the building and preparing the float. We decided to rent a low wagon and have a platform built on it, at least ten by thirty feet. This was to be decorated so it would look like a bar room of a saloon, by putting a bar on the float and having one or more bartenders serving beer. I asked him if he intended putting the large plate mirror behind the bar, and he said, "sure, we have two or three back bars stored in the warehouse." I realized that this would never do, so I asked him what kind of horses he intended using to pull the float and he said they would use four or six of the horses which were used to pulling the trucks. I knew that these horses had plenty of life in them and that they might get frightened from the scent of Buster, so I told him I did not think it was a good idea to have the mirror on the float as it might get thrown off or knocked down and injure someone, so that was thrown out of the idea.

Mr. Brooks asked if there wasn't something we could use to kill the scent of Buster but I told them I knew of nothing, unless it would be the perfume of a skunk and was sure that this would not do. They got quite a laugh out of that but said they were sure that there must be something we could use. I then remembered that we might use some asafetida to rub on Buster, for when I was a youngster my mother used to put a little of this in a small sack and tie it around my neck. She said it would keep me from catching any diseases, but as it smelled so bad, I used to take it off and hide it before I went to school and then before I got home, I would put it on. Mr. Bates and Mr. Brooks both thought that this would do the trick so I told them that I thought it was worth a try before we entered the parade. I figured it would be best to take Buster over to the barnyard where the horses were kept and lead Buster around the yard and see just how the horses acted and see if they became excited when they got Busters scent. We would have to get them used to him before we dare put Buster upon the float for they might run away and do much damage.

We finally agreed that it was best not to put the bar on the float but that the large round table would be alright and we would decorate the float with all kinds of different shrubs we could find in the Wichita Mountains along the streams. Mr. Bates told Mr. Brooks and I to go right ahead and build the float to suit ourselves.

Mr. Brooks suggested that I go out and see what luck I would have in renting a low wheeled wagon, so I started out but was not very successful and reported to Mr. Brooks just what I had found. The Rickley Hardware store had one or more new ones in stock and I felt that we might be able to rent one of those, so it was up to me to go next morning and find out just what the verdict might be. I went there the first thing next morning and was told that it would be alright for me to use the wagon and if the wagon was brought back in good condition, there would be no charges for the use of it. I then asked them if they would furnish me a man to help set the wagon up, as it was not yet assembled, also that the brewery company would be glad to stand all expense.

Inside of three hours we had the wagon down to the blacksmith shop, having a large frame built on it and in a day or so it was all completed. I figured they had put at least fifty percent more lumber in the frame than was necessary but Mr. Brooks said that it should be more substantial as he could sell it very easily afterwards. Several men with myself pushed the wagon over to the barnyard, where we intended decorating it.

I then told Mr. Brooks that I had better go get Buster and take him over to the barnyard but he advised me to wait until evening as most of the horses were out on deliveries and if they found Buster in the yard when brought in, they would become frightened, so I decided to bring him over in the evening after dinner.

Well the fun began after dinner when we took Buster over for it was but a few minutes until the horses became aware of some strange scent and they began to snort and paw the floor and try to break their halter rope, so we decided that the next time we took him over, it would be best to try out the asafetida and see if that would help any so I went to the drug store and got some asafetida and rubbed it all over Buster as I wanted to tie Buster in the yard near the barn, as I thought that the horses would finally get used to having him around. Mr. Brooks advised me to be there early in the morning to get Buster away from there before the drivers brought the horses out so I followed his instructions and was there before six o'clock but the horses did not seem to be very excited, of course they snorted and jumped around a bit. I continued to leave Buster in the barnyard and it was only a day or so until they were used to having him there.

As we only had a few days more, we had to begin to get our decorations together. The first thing we did was to get the large table, which we put in the center of the float, this was made stationary to the frame. We had to locate six large arm chairs, which was not too hard to do as most of the saloons or gambling houses had them. I was very much in doubt if Buster could sit in one of them or if it would be substantial enough as he was weighing over a thousand pounds, so I suggested to Mr. Brooks that it would be best to make a similar chair but make it considerable heavier and somewhat larger, so I quickly located a carpenter shop, I drew a rough sketch of what I wanted and left it with him, saying that we must have it in a day or so and when it was finished, he brought it up to the distributing house and I will say, he surely did a real job. I took the chair over to the barnyard, where I had Buster chained. I thought it would be a good idea to start training Buster to sit in the chair as this was one of the tricks I had never taught him to do. I had no trouble in getting him to sit in the chair though and I gave him a bottle of sweetened water. I then took the chair on the wagon frame and also Buster on the frame and had him sit in the chair so that we would know just how far the chair had to be from the table and we found out that we had to slide the chair at least two feet from the table in order for Buster to get into it but by the time Buster got into the chair we could not slide it up to the table, so we decided that the best plans was to make the chair stationary and have Buster get into it and then push the table up to him. It took us considerable longer getting the tables and chairs all set just where we wanted them. It surely looked comical to see Buster upon the wagon sitting in that big chair all by himself and I really think that Buster knew we were laughing at him for he seemed to turn his head from one side to the other and stick out his tongue.

My next problem was to find the men who would sit in these chairs around the table with Buster. You might think it was an easy proposition but it was very difficult. I will never forget the first two men I interviewed, one was full blooded Indian and the other was a half breed Indian. I told them to be at the barnyard of the Brewery Company in an hour and both said that they would. I then located some personal friends of mine and they also told me they would accept and would be down to the yard as soon as possible as I wished to have a rehearsal. When I got back to the yard, the two Indians were there and were sitting about fifty feet from Buster, talking to each other in their own language, which I did not understand. In a few minutes my friends arrived on the scene, so I took Buster on the wagon and placed him in his chair and fed him several pieces of candy. I then told the men to be seated at the table for Mr. Brooks and several others wanted to get the idea as to how it would look. Three of the men climbed on the wagon to get in their chairs but one of the Indians was making his way to the street, shaking his head and waving his hand at me. Of course I did not hear what he said but I can imagine what he thought when I told him that he had to get on the wagon and sit next to Buster.

I then invited Mr. Brooks to take the Indians place and as he came up on the wagon he asked one of the other men to exchange chairs as it was a bit hard for him to make up his mind but he finally did. One of my friends asked me where Buster's muzzle was and I asked him if he was getting cold feet, but he thought it would be much better for all of them if Buster had it on. I told them that I did not like to start putting the muzzle on him as it would have to be taken off the day of the parade as I intended serving him sweetened water out of a beer bottle but the men would be served cold beer, but not too much.

Mr. Bates then explained to them just what he would pay for the two or three hours of work in the parade and they were more than pleased with his offer, which was five dollars each, for at that time five dollars was a large amount of money. I asked Mr. Brooks if I could have two of them go with me to get the decorations for the float which he consented to.

Most of the next day was spent in getting the decorations which consisted of hundreds of sunflowers, branches from mesquite trees, oak, wild plum and several other trees which I have forgotten their names. With all of them we had a large wagon load with which Mr. Brooks was well pleased as there was only one more day between us and the parade so we started to decorate the float the next morning. As there were four or five of us working on the decorating of the float, it did not take over six or seven hours to complete.

That afternoon, Mr. Bates and three other gentlemen arrived from Oklahoma City and of course were anxious to see the float, also to give us some assistance, providing that we needed any. They were certainly enthused over the float and I heard one of them mention that it would be a knock out, wherever I went for an exhibit. Orders were given to all working on the job to be there by six o'clock the next morning, as you know there is always plenty to be done the last minute before entering the float in the parade.

I could scarcely wait until the next morning as I was as excited as a child and wasted no time in getting there early. The first thing I noticed when I came to the gate of the barnyard, there were eight head of horses tied across the street, which I figured had come from some livery stable or ranch. When I met one of the teamsters, I asked him what all of the live stock was doing across the street and he said that they had to get extra stock to take the place of the ones they were using in the parade, also that they would to put on extra wagons to take care of their customers. They said that the stock should have been hooked up before then but that they had been unable to get them into the yard on account of Buster. I then told him that his hands were not tied, why had he not unsnapped the chain and lead Buster back to his cage where I usually kept him. He sort of laughed and said, "I'll tell you, this Brewery Company hired me as a teamster, not to lead bears around. If I had my way about it, that bear would not have been left here in this yard for I have not had my mind on my business since he had been in this yard." "Are you really afraid of Buster?" "I would certainly like to see the man who is not afraid of an animal like that one. You might not be, but you are only one out of many."

"Why don't you come over and pet him, I'll show you he won't hurt you." I had to do plenty of talking and finally he decided to come over and give him a pat or so but keeping his body as far away from Buster as possible and after doing so he said, "Why he won't hurt you will he, well I can tell everyone that I have petted Buster on the head." I told him that I would take Buster to his cage, which was about three blocks away and then they could go ahead and get ready for their deliveries. Even after I had taken Buster away, they still had a hard time in getting those new horses in the yard so as to hitch them to the wagons.

As soon as the delivery wagons were cleared out of the yard, I brought Buster back to the yard. They had three span of horses ready to hook up to the float and I have never seen finer looking horses in my life. They had taken several hundred of the smaller sunflowers and many yards of blue silk ribbon and decorated the horses. The four men and myself who were to be on the float, were dressed as Westerners, wearing large cowboy hats, very bright colored shirts, belts and holsters carrying shells and guns, also boots with spurs. Of course the guns carried no shells except the one I was carrying, as I always made it a habit to have one handy in case I should need it as Buster might get vicious and hurt or even try to kill someone and the only thing I could do would be to kill him, of course I was always praying that a time like that would never come.

We hitched the horses up to the float and drove it out of the yard to join the parade but I did not put Buster on the float as I knew he would get too restless and tired before the parade got under way. I had rubbed Buster with plenty of asafetida, trying to kill the scent. As all of the floats were pulled by teams of horses and there would also be hundreds of horses in town, I certainly did not want to cause a lot of these horses to run away and hurt someone, so I took this precaution.

Our float was such a beautiful looking float, so they decided to have us lead the floats or right behind the first band which was in the lead and several of the band boys asked me if I had Buster chained for if he should get loose, there would be no band playing but I told them not to worry.

Mr. Bates and Mr. Brooks came by and said they wished to give me my final orders as to what I was to do after the parade. They gave me a list of all the saloons in town which handled their beer, there being about twenty-five or thirty. "Now we want you and Buster, also the rest of the boys to go along with you, going from one saloon to another and order the bartenders to treat every man in the house, except minors, to a pint bottle of their beer. The bartenders were to keep track of all the beer served and will hand me the bill for the amount of bottles served and the company in turn will refund the saloon at retail prices."

After receiving my final instructions, I was ready to take Buster on the float and I told Mr. Bates that Buster might get a bit restless from all of the noise and the band playing but if I had enough room I might be able to put Buster through some of his tricks but there seemed to be so many cases of beer that it was pretty small space to try.

Buster was now going back and forth on the float and also raising up once in a while so Mr. Bates began to worry and thought that Buster was already tired but I told him not to worry as Buster often did this and as soon as I put him in his chair and got started that he would be alright. I then instructed the rest of the men, that if Buster should by any chance get on a rampage, not to get frightened but just sit still for I would be able to quiet him down. One of the men spike up and said, "Now if that brute gets angry or does any funny tricks, I am leaving this float just as fast as my feet can take me off."

"Now just don't get excited for everything is going to be alright." In a few minutes the parade began to push forward and as we were several blocks from the main street of the town, it took ten or fifteen minutes to get to where most of the people were standing.

As the band began to play, Buster seemed to get quite a kick out of the music so at once I gave him some candy and in that way had no trouble in getting him into the chair. I then asked one of the men to hand me one of the bottles of sweetened water which we had put in one of the cases under the table. These bottles all had caps on them just as though they were filled with beer. The young man who handed me the bottle started to take the cap off but I told him it was not necessary as Buster liked to take the cap off of his own bottles and after he had a taste of his sweetened water, the cheering crowd did not seem to bother him.

About this time the four men who were standing at each corner of the float began to pull of the caps of the ice cold beer and hand it out to the public, and you should have been the hands out for beer. To my recollection it was a real warm day and the ice cold beer was in keeping with the weather. It seemed as though there must be a thousand people following this float and as we entered the business section of the town, the crowd became much larger and I had no idea that there were so many people in Kiowa County.

After going through the first block of the large crowd, some men stepped up to the float and said that Mr. Bates sent word that everything was going over great but would it be possible for me to start Buster to do some of his tricks. I then advised some of the men to try to make more room by moving back some of the empty beer cases.

There were several cowboys standing close to the float and two of them pulled out their revolvers and began to shoot up in the air and I was afraid that they might take a shot at Buster if they had many more drinks but they soon quieted down as I told them that I was going to put Buster through some of his stunts. First I made him stand up on his hind legs and do his dance as the band was playing and he was so much better at it when he had music, then I made him get down and I got on his back and by pulling on his collar, he would rare up with me just as a horse does. There was so much cheering and yelling I thought that I better get him back in his chair and give him another bottle of sweetened water. We had just turned the first corner of the City Square where I had Buster do his stunts and after I got Buster back in his place, one of the men said that he would not put his arms around that bear like I did and I told him to just wait until we got to the next corner of the Square and I would how him a real trick.

While I was putting Buster through his stunts the float must not have moved over a hundred feet and there was no beer being given away as all the men were all watching Buster but as the float began to move on the beer began to be passed out very fast and I must say it surely kept the four men busy opening all of these bottles. Naturally some of the beer ran out of the bottles and blew over the float so that there was no scent of asafetida, it really smelled more like a brewery.

Just before we came to the next turn, Mr. Bates came up to the float and called me over to him so that I could hear him, saying that the judges were at the next corner and for me to put Buster through some of his best stunts. He also said that our float was drawing all the attention of the crowd and there was no reason why we should not receive the first prize, so do your best and if we do get the first prize, I will see that you get a good tailor made suit out of it. This surely sounded good to me and I told him to just watch us at the next corner for it would be good.

Buster seemed to be in the best of humor as he was full of candy and sweetened water. I took him out of his chair and had him stand up and dance again and by the time he was through we were at the next corner and the float had stopped. There was so much hollering and cheering that I had to scream as loud as I could, that if they would be just a little quieter, I would put Buster through one of his most dangerous stunts. They finally did quiet down to a certain extent, I told them a little about Buster the Silver Tip Grizzly and I then took him by his upper and lower jaw, opening his mouth as wide as I could get it, doing this several times, so that the crowd could get the idea as to the size of his mouth. I then made Buster open his mouth of his own accord and stuck my head in his mouth several inches. This was done twice very successfully and at this time a man came close to the float and said, "You are taking some awful chances, young fellow." But nevertheless I received plenty of applause and cheering.

As the float began to move on, Mr. Bates ran up to the float and asked me not to do that again. We continued on down the block to the next turn around the square, giving beer away as fast as we could snap off the caps, so when we arrived at the turn, I made Buster get up and dance again, then to lie down on his back between his feet. I then had him stand up on his front paws, like a person standing on his hands. By that time I was getting short of candy, as every time I had Buster do his tricks, I had to feed him several pieces.

By the time we arrived at the next corner, which was the last one around the square, the hollering was so great, that we could not hear each other talk and I was glad that we only had two more blocks to go as I was getting uneasy about the boys at the table for they had been drinking quite a lot of beer and I was afraid that they were getting under the influence of it and I knew I would need help when I came to the end of the parade.

When we finally reached the end, there waiting for us were Mr. Brooks and Mr. Bates and several of the Brewery Company's men and they surely gave me a wonderful reception. Mr. Bates then asked me to have dinner with him before I started out with the bear, as I was to go from saloon to saloon with Buster. I accepted the invitation and we went to a restaurant which was close by, asking the proprietor to serve us at once. While eating our dinner, as the noon day meal was called in those days, Mr. Bates told me that our float had received the first prize and the offer he had made me was still good. I was certainly thrilled when I heard this for I was sure of a great success at this advertising.

After we had finished dinner, I went over to get Buster as I had him chained to the float and I led him right up the middle of the street with several hundred people following, so the first saloon I came to, I stopped out in front and announced to all, that they were welcome to get a free bottle of beer, that the treat was on me. Of course it was like a stampede of cattle, the way they went into that saloon but at that they kept their distance from Buster who was standing close to the door. It was not long until the place was packed and I did not stay long here as I had many places to go, so as soon as all were treated and I got my bill, I started for the next saloon and I did not have far to go as to my remembrance there were five or six saloons in one block and at least four of them handled the beer I was advertising, I managed to get all of the saloons in this block but by this time it seemed to be advertised all over town that if you would go with the fellow who has the grizzly bear, he will treat you to beer in each saloon.

I remember one saloon I came out of, was right close to the corner of the Court House Square, at this time I could scarcely make up my mind which way to go for every way I looked I could see hundreds of people.

I did not have much difficulty in getting through the crowd as they would all make room for Buster. Of course I put Buster's muzzle on as I knew it would be too dangerous to lead him through such a crowd without it. I was soon across the street and starting down the next block taking in all of the saloons and treating all to beer. I also put Buster through some of his tricks in these saloons which attracted plenty of attention.

By the time we had made it into ten or twelve saloons, one of the bartenders asked me if Buster would like a bottle of beer. I told him that he did not care much for beer but that he would drink it. I took Buster's muzzle off and had him stand up to the bar, thinking that perhaps he would enjoy a bottle of cold beer as I knew he needed a drink of some kind after all he had gone through the past few hours. The bartender handed me a bottle of beer, the cap having been removed and I was greatly surprised how much Buster seemed to enjoy this bottle of beer, but it was not long until I noticed that Buster began to get drowsy and wanted to lie down and also two of the men with me were beginning to feel the same way as we had all indulged in several bottles of beer.

I thought that it was best to get Buster outside but I had no more than gotten him to the middle of the sidewalk when Buster gave up and fell to the walk. As the day was so warm, the men who were with me as well as myself, tried to keep the crowd back from Buster, so that he could get air as he was so fat at this time. I had weighed him just a few days before and he tipped the scale at one thousand and fifty pounds.

It was but a short time until the City Marshal stepped up to me and said "You will have to get that bear off the street because it is causing too much excitement and the crowds are too large."

I was feeling pretty good so I just up and said, "Well there he is, you have my permission to move him if you want to."

Now I began to realize that this one bottle of beer had not put Buster in this condition and that it must have been framed up with the bartender to have put some strong liquor into this beer bottle, probably rock and rye and as Buster had had nothing to eat, only the sweetened water on the float this surely put him down and out. As Buster lay there stretched out on the sidewalk, I could not make up my mind just what to do as I had tried everything I knew, to get him up on his feet but there seemed to be no hope of this.

About this time Mr. Bates and Mr. Brooks came on the scene and as I was a bit tipsy myself, I tried to keep from showing it to them so Mr. Brooks suggested to me that I had better get Buster back to his cage, in some way or another, also said that he had done a good days work and that they were more than satisfied.

I then told one of the men who was with me, to go get an expressman and wagon and perhaps we could manage to get him in the wagon and in that way get him back to his cage.

During all this time someone had spread the news that Buster had been shot and killed and of course that caused plenty of excitement. He might as well have been killed for he would have been no more unconscious than he was in his present condition, and as for myself, by this time, I did not know if I had one or two bears.

It was but a short time until the man came back with the expressman and wagon and I told the expressman to just back his wagon up to the sidewalk as the sidewalks were nearly as high as the express wagon and most of them were boardwalks.

We had very little difficulty in getting Buster in the wagon as there were five or six men who took hold of him, some taking hold of his chain, others his feet and any place they could hold and we finally dragged him into the wagon. Of course many of these men would never have gotten within fifteen feet of this bear, had they been sober. I really think that some of them thought that Buster was dead.

Now I gave the expressman instructions just where to deliver him, which was about four or five blocks away. As the express wagon was a small spring wagon, the two men and myself decided to walk along side of the wagon and we also figured that the walk would do us some good. But the expressman had no more than let his brake loose on the wagon, until the team got the scent of the bear and caused them to run away. If I remember rightly, it was not over two hundred feet to the first culvert and the way these were built here, they were used as a drain, sort of a small bridge but raised above the real surface of the street about eight or ten inches, so when the wagon carrying Buster hit this culvert, it threw Buster up in the air and when he came down the wagon was gone as the team was traveling so fast. So down came Buster in the middle of the street. I was not far away when this happened and it did not worry me as to Buster getting hurt but I was worried about the team running away as it might run over someone or even kill someone. The old fellow who was driving the team held his head, for about half way down the next block there was a vacant lot and in front of this lot the sidewalk was not very high, so he managed to turn the team over this sidewalk and into the vacant lot, but in doing this the back wheels and frame of the wagon were left in the street while the front wheels went with the team.

I learned the following day that the old gentleman who drove the wagon was not hurt in any way and that the Brewery Company was to have the wagon built over so that it would be better than it had been before this happened.

Well coming back to Buster, here he lay sprawled out in the middle of the street and this fall had not wakened him. We still had the problem to solve how to get him back to his cage.

Someone in the crowd suggested that we get a large wheelbarrow and try to haul him in that. There was a hardware store close by, so we got one of the kind which is used to haul brick. I distinctly remember that when the boy brought it over, it looked like two wheelbarrows, so you can see what effect the beer and the hot sun was having on me and it was not only myself, but the rest of the fellows. I had no trouble whatsoever in getting plenty of help in lifting Buster into the wheelbarrow as all were under the influence of the beer. When I asked them to grab hold and give me a lift, there were so many that they were in each others way. I advised some of them to take his front legs and some his hind legs and I would try to hold his head up. We finally did get him into the wheelbarrow and as some would try to steady it, two of the men tried to push it but we would no more than get fifty of seventy-five feet, when over would go Buster and all on top of him. Well this was certainly a side show for the people looking on and I guess they got their moneys worth out of it.

We must have loaded Buster into this wheelbarrow at least ten times or more and each time all would fall on top of Buster. I know that I would have had no help if they had been sober. Of course the crowd was so large that the streets were filled as well as all the sidewalks and there were three or four deputies trying to keep the crowds back so that we could proceed with Buster. At last we managed to get him as far as the railroad tracks, which were still a good block away from his cage. The first track we came to was a switch track and as I knew that I was not able to stand on my feet much longer, I tied Buster's chain to the track. I remember very well that there was a refrigerator car real close and I knew that this would make some shade for Buster while he rested.

It was not long until I was down and out, someone picked me up and carried me to the Central Hotel and I did not know anything until the next morning. This was my first offense of being intoxicated and I made a promise that it would be my last.

The first thing which came into my mind the next morning, was what had become of Buster. There was a friend of mine in the room when I woke up and he told me that Buster was alright but that he thought it would do me good to get up and stir around also go down and move Buster as I had tied him to the railroad track. I managed to get up and get my clothes on but I was still dizzy and nauseated even after I went out doors, so I stopped in a drug store and got something which helped me considerable.

I went directly to the railroad tracks and what a funny scene was before me. There was Buster pacing back and forth as fast as he could go, looking at no one. Quite a crowd of people were watching him, but the funniest thing was, when I went up to untie the chain from the tracks, there lay two of the boys, who had helped me, under the refrigerator car. I went over and shook one of them and told him that a switch engine was going to hook onto that car and unless they got out from under there, it would run over them. As they raised up and looked around and saw Buster on the rampage, they lost no time in moving.

Buster did not seem glad to see me or anyone else after being on that spree. There is no doubt but that he was feeling a little like the rest of us and wanted to be left alone. I untied him from the tracks and started with him toward his cage and had no trouble as I must say, he lead me. He surely made fast tracks in getting to his cage and as soon as I unlocked the gate to the cage, he went right down into the cave, I guess he was ashamed of himself and wanted to hide after his experience of the previous day and there were probably many people who felt like doing the same thing.

As my agreement with the Brewery Company was satisfactorily filled at this Carnival, I had to prepare to move Buster to the next town where we were to put on an exhibition in the next few days. This town was Rainy Mountain, which was about fifty miles from Hobart.

I had just completed a new crate for Buster, which was mostly made of steel and iron. I was proud of this crate as it was so well built and looked so good.

After taking the crate to the depot, I then lead Buster down and put him in it. When the train pulled in there were several hundred people at the station to tell me goodby and wish me luck, many telling me to be careful as I was taking some mighty big chances with Buster. Of course I had quite a feeling of pride in being given the opportunity to exhibit Buster on these occasions.

When we started to load Buster into the express car, we discovered that the crate with Buster in it, was too heavy to lift, so I took Buster out and loaded the empty crate, then leading Buster in the car and into his crate, and in a few minutes the train pulled out of the station and we were on our way to Rainy Mountain.

It did not take long to get to Rainy Mountain and as soon as I arrived, I had to look for a place in which I could take Buster out of his crate, also where the public would be safe. I finally located a place in the rear of a lumber yard, where he had plenty of room to get some exercise and as there was a high fence all around this yard, he was well protected.

I do not exactly remember just what this celebration was to commemorate but it had something to do with the Indians. There must have been two thousand Indians in the town besides all the white people. There was to be no parade in this small town but I was to put Buster through some of his stunts, several times a day, out in the streets and also in front of the saloons.

I went to the lumber yard to get Buster so I could start him out on his second exhibition. While putting him through his tricks, the old squaws and Indian children would sit right down in the middle of the street and seemed to get such a kick out of it. I took Buster into the saloons and treated the people to beer as I had done in Hobart.

There was plenty of grunting and pow-wowing by the Indians but I was not able to understand them. I noticed in particular that most every Indian buck, squaw and child had a sack of peanuts and I never in my life saw so many peanut shells as were in those streets. They all seemed to enjoy themselves and wherever I would take Buster, they would follow right along with us and wanting me to make Buster do more tricks.

I had engagements in several other towns close by but I will not go into detail as they were all on the same principal and all performances seemed to be very successful.

On one occasion, I remember taking Buster out of his crate and was leading him through the town, when he either became frightened or someone threw a rock at him, as there was a large crowd following us and I think that someone wanted to see just what he would do if excited. Well he jerked loose from me and started right back toward the depot where his crate was standing. It is pretty hard to explain just what happened as there was plenty of screaming and yelling, some falling down and this helped to frighten him more. I remember in particular that there was a young man who started running down the street, in the same direction Buster was going but he was in front of Buster and when he looked back and saw Buster right behind him, he saw that he was not going fast enough, so he pulled his hat off and I really do not think a race horse could have caught up with him. Of course he thought Buster was after him, but he wasn't, he was on his way to the crate. If the young man turned off into one of the side streets, Buster would have gone right on down the street. The young man kept right on running for over a block after Buster stopped at the depot. We all certainly got a good laugh out of this and the young man was kidded plenty about it, but he did not consider it a laughing matter, as it took him quite some time to get over his scare.

I hurried to the depot where Buster had gone and did not get mad at him but fed him some candy and in this way I got him quieted down. I then felt all over him to see if someone had thrown something at him which had stuck in his fur and was hurting him but I could find nothing. I thought perhaps one of the boys had played a joke on him but never found out what it was.

The crowd had thinned out considerably, so I thought it best to keep Buster in his crate for a while, so I went to a store and bought him some apples to eat while he was waiting.

After an hour or so, I got Buster to go up into town where I had a place to keep him. I had no trouble leading him this time even though there was a large crowd but no jokes were tried on him either. We put on a very good performance at this town and received a great write up in the papers.

Several weeks rolled by and it was not long until I was on my way back to Hobart, Oklahoma, my home town. Everyone seemed glad to see me come home and that I was still alive. Many questions were asked and they wanted me to tell of my experiences on this trip.

It was now getting late in the fall and Buster was about ready to enter his cave for his long rest and sleep. He seemed so glade to once again be in his large cage where he had plenty of room to move about as he pleased.

During the holidays of this year, my sister and her husband came from California to make us a visit and of course were very anxious to see Buster as they had not seen him since he was a little fellow, weighing about four hundred pounds. I told them that he had gained about six hundred pounds and that they would not recognize him, also that he had been in his cave for about two months and that I was very much in doubt as to whether I could get him to come out as he did not like to be disturbed.

We went down to the cage and I went in and took hold of the chain and tried to pull him out and at the same time he jerked the chain and gave a loud growl. As it was very dark down there in the cave, I thought I might take a lantern down in the cave and in this way my sister and husband could get a look at him. I got a lantern and started down into the cave, holding the lantern as far in front of me as I could, so as to locate Buster. I had not gone very far until Buster hit the lantern with one of his paws. Now maybe you think I tarried down there, well I didn't as I made tracks out of there as fast as I could and all that I had left of the lantern was the handle. I was afraid that this might cause a fire down in the cave but it did not. My brother-in-law suggested that I leave him alone but I told him

I intended to get him out if there was any possible way of doing it. My father had a large span of mules, so I hitched them up to the wagon and took it over to the cave, backing it up to the cave and taking a heavy chain and fastening on to Buster's chain, then fastening this to the axle of the wagon. I figured there would be no trouble in getting him out this way. Now this team got right down and pulled but Buster did not come out so I became afraid that I might hurt him in some way. He seemed to have as much strength as the team but of course he must have braced himself against the sides of the cave. I finally unhooked the chain and called down to Buster to just stay down there and starve to death if he wanted to.

My sister and husband got a kick out of this and much disappointed in not getting to see Buster as they had come such a long distance.

I then told them I was planning on my own road show as I had planned it the year before but that I had such a good offer from the Brewing Company, I had postponed until this year. I told them that I might be out in California someday and then they would have a chance to see Buster. My brother-in-law warned me to be very careful as Buster was getting older and so powerful and that he might turn on me at any time. They had to leave without seeing him.

It was now nearing the time when Buster would be coming out of the cave, so I would make a trip down to the cage every day or so to see if he was out. It was about the first of March when a friend of mine met me on the street and told me that he had seen Buster out in his cage so I rushed right over to the cage and sure enough, there was Buster. I got my key out and unlocked the gate and then hesitated as I had no candy with me so I thought I better protect myself with some as it had been three months since I had seen him.

I also had my good clothes on, so thought I better change to some old ones. I also got my revolver and some candy. After doing this I was ready to enter the cage, but just the same I was a bit shy, but Buster came right over and began to smell my shoes. I offered him some candy but he would not take it, he just looked up at me with his one eye as much as to say, don't bother me with things like that. I patted him on the head and finally got him to raise up and put his paws on my shoulders. He seemed to recognize my scent and gave me a lick on the cheek. Nevertheless I was not feeling very anxious to play with him as I guess I had lost some of my nerve during the winter months. I soon stepped out of the cage and left Buster to figure it out by himself. I would go back to the cage at least once or twice a day trying to get him to eat something.

I noticed one queer thing about his front paws, after taking this long nap, that the hair was all off of his toes and back about an inch and half on the upper part of his paws, I learned later that this was caused by licking between his toes during his hibernation. This seemed to furnish him with nourishment or form a saliva in his mouth which he needed.

After Buster had been out of the cave some time and was once again like himself, it was time for me to begin to put him through his training for I was sure that he had forgotten some of his tricks and I knew I must get him ready for my road show. In a few weeks I decided to take Buster out to the Park again. I think I mentioned to you before that the Park is where I kept Buster during the summer months or early spring. It was here I began to train Buster and you would be surprised how little of the tricks I had taught him, he had forgotten. It was not long until he was almost as good as the fall before.

I learned that there was to be a three day celebration in Mangum, Oklahoma so I went in search of my friend who had helped me put on the dog and bear fight, which never came off. I told him about the celebration and asked him if he would like to go in with me putting on a show there. He was very much in favor, so we got on the train and went to Mangum, to see if we could enter our bear show in the celebration. We finally got to talk to some of the big men of the town and told them just what our show consisted of and in fact one of the men had seen Buster so he knew just what to expect. They decided to give us a permit to exhibit our show, providing we built a large wire cage, this we agreed to do. The fee was to be ten dollars per day, which we considered reasonable.

After getting this all settled, the next move was to locate a place where we could put our show. While walking down to the Hotel, we passed a vacant lot which was between two brick buildings. I said perhaps we could lease this lot very reasonable and why couldn't we get several wagon covers and fasten them together and put up between these buildings in both front and rear and could lease some lumber from the lumber yard to make a few seats and a platform so the next thing was to locate the owner of the lot and make necessary arrangements. This did not take us very long as luck seemed to be with us so now that all was settled, we hurried home to make ready for our move to Mangum.

The first thing we did was to have a large sign made on which we had a large painting of Buster. The canvas on which the sign was made, was about twenty feet by eighteen feet. This we had made in Oklahoma City and also the painting was done there. Buster's picture was painted in a silver color and under it were the words, "The Only Trained Silver Tip Grizzly Bear in Captivity, weighing over One Thousand Pounds." This canvas and the artists work was very expensive but was surely worth the money and was really fifty percent better than we had expected it to be.

We only had about two weeks to get ready so of course I kept Buster busy putting him through his stunts twice a day. Buster had just finished shedding and his new coat of fur was certainly beautiful, it was just full of silver and looked a great deal like a silver fox.

After debating, we decided that the best way to take Buster to Mangum, was by wagon. I took one of my father's mule teams and wagon and loaded everything on, putting Buster in the crate which I had used the previous summer. We allowed ourselves five days to get there and get things fixed up for the show. I remember it took us two long days to drive this distance and in one of the towns we passed through, we took Buster out of his crate and gave a small performance on the street, putting him through several of his tricks and afterwards passed the hat around and took up a collection. I do not remember the amount of money we received but I do remember that it was enough to pay our expenses to Mangum and back. These few dollars sure looked good to us as our capital was getting low for we had been out quite a lot of money in making our preparations for this show.

The next town we passed through was Granite but we did not give a performance here for after talking it over, we decided that there would be many of the people from here who would go to Mangum for the celebration, and we figured that we could get ten to twenty-five cents from them there.

We camped on the outskirts of town that night and was up and on our way by daybreak as we wanted to get into Mangum early that evening, which we did. We had no trouble on our trip, everything worked just like clockwork.

As our tickets and passes had been made in Hobart, I suggested that we give several passes away to the hotels and restaurants so that we could get food free for Buster and perhaps we could get some of our own meals in that way. There were three or four hotels and eight to ten restaurants, so we went up town the next morning to get our breakfast, the first one we went into, I asked him if we could trade him four passes to our show for our breakfast and some food for Buster. I told him if the show was not worth the money, all he had to do, was to come to me and say so and his money would be refunded to him. He accepted and certainly gave us a good breakfast and said that if we would come back in an hour or so, he would save us the scraps for Buster.

I then went to the hotel just across the street and put the same proposition to the hotel proprietor. He seemed very pleased, so we gave him eight passes for which we were to receive several meals. We had no trouble in getting plenty of food for Buster as all we had to do was to give the cook or dishwasher a pass and they would save really too much.

During all the time we spent in Mangum, which was six days, we did not spend a cent for food. It is a good thing we had plenty of passes as we also traded them for hay and corn for the mules also giving passes to the men who helped build the wire cage on the stage. Of course we could not give enough passes to cover the cost of renting the lumber but we gave enough that it did not cost us too much.

It did not take these men long to build enough seats to seat about three hundred people, also the stage and cage which was about twenty feet square. I also had a small platform built out in front which was about four or five feet wide, seven feet long and five feet high. We put our canvas in the rear of this platform with our large sign in front in center and everything was ready for our first performance.

We talked it over and thought it would be a good idea to go to the Courthouse and invite the Mayor, Sheriff and Marshals and some of the people who worked for the county, to a special show which we planned to give that evening about seven thirty. I figured this would also be sort of a rehearsal and we would be ready for the opening the next day. Now maybe you think I didn't put on a show for the guests that evening. There were about twenty five people who witnessed this first show and they surely gave me much encouragement, telling me how they had enjoyed it and the Mayor said that no one could afford to miss a show like this for twenty-five cents.

The next morning we were up real early and we were surprised to see how many buggies, wagons and people horse back, already in town, ready to start the three day celebration.

Our fist performance was to start at eleven a.m., so the first thing I did was to dress in some very old clothes, having on a white shirt which was torn badly on sleeves and back. We had also taken some blood which we put on the shirt in several places to make them think that it was caused by Buster, scratching me with his claws. Of course this drew the attention of the public, I was pretty husky in those days, weighing about one hundred seventy pounds with very large muscles and was very strong.

I took Buster out on the small platform which I had built out in front and as Mr. Powell had a megaphone, he began to call out, "See Buster the SILVER TIP GRIZZLY BEAR, the largest and only one in captivity which is trained. We are giving the best show for the money and if you are not satisfied, we will return your money. Right this way, Hurry, Hurry."

It was not long until we had many gathered around the platform as we had informed them that we were giving a free exhibit to all. I spoke a few minutes telling where Buster was captured and how long it took to train him. The people stood back quite some distance from the platform as they were afraid that Buster would get loose. I had him stand up on his hind feet and shake hands with me, put his paws on my shoulder and love me, then stand on his front paws. I then took Buster's upper and lower jaw in my hands and opened his mouth, showing them how large it was and explained to them that I would give them a real thrill inside the tent by putting my head in his mouth, also that to my knowledge, there had never been a bear trainer who had accomplished this trick. The admission to the show is twenty-five cents for adults and ten cents for children and if you like the show and really enjoy it, tell everyone not to miss seeing this show of Buster the Silver Tip Grizzly. If you are not pleased with the show and feel that you did not get your moneys worth, I will be glad to refund it to you.

Buster was then taken inside the tent and put in the cage. I came out to help Powell as he was selling the tickets and had also hired a young man to collect them. No doubt but that you readers have all been to a side show and know how the crowds rush in for tickets, so as to get in and get a good seat. Well that is just what was happening and I saw that Powell could not sell the tickets half fast enough, so I jumped up on the other side of the box on which he was standing and began to help him. After selling about three hundred or more, I explained that there were no more seats and if they went in now, they would have to stand up, but there would be another show, one at two p.m. and another at four p.m. and there was not use to go in and stand up, as they could go in later and get a seat. Even after all of that talking, we could not stop selling tickets as some were determined to go in but finally we just left the box and closed the canvas and had the young man watch the entrance.

The next thing was to put on our very best show as we wanted to keep on getting such crowds for the next three days.

I entered the wire cage in which I put Buster through his tricks. I gave a short speech as to how and where Buster was captured, the difference between Buster and the ordinary brown or black bear and other things I have already mentioned. Buster was then put through twelve to fifteen tricks and between each act, I would explain how I trained him to do these stunts. Buster was rewarded with much applause after each trick and he seemed to realize that the public liked it. Up to this time we had spent about an hour and twenty minutes and was then ready to put on my last stunt, wrestling with Buster. I told them how strong I was and for them not to bet money on Buster throwing me, but of course I knew that he could throw ten men like me but I knew the trick which would throw him, so I was safe.

After making Buster rare up on his hind feet and back up several times, trying all the time to catch hold of him under his shoulder blades, and in doing this, I would shove him around, first one way and then another and get my right arm pretty well around toward his back and with my left arm I would put it around his front paws and would try to throw him off his feet but failed. I would then pull away from him to rest for a few seconds making out that I was tired and when I went back I had a corn husker in the center of my hand of course keeping this hid from the public, I would wrestle a little while and would then reach up under his collar and use the husker which would pinch and hurt him, so in this way I had no trouble whatsoever in throwing him. After he fell to the floor, I would sit on his stomach and endeavor to hold him down. I had to be mighty careful in doing this for sometimes he would raise his hind feet and catch me in the seat of the pants and that meant a new pair of pants or else get a tailor to mend them.

After this stunt was finished, I invited anyone in the audience to come up and wrestle with Buster and throw him off his feet. If they did so I would give them twenty five dollars and also guarantee that Buster would not hurt them in any way. They all seemed to get quite a kick out of this but I noticed that no one came up and took my offer.

I then made Buster get up and make several bows to the audience and I thanked all of them, saying that if they were not satisfied with the show, their money would be refunded, but if they liked the show, please tell all of your friends that they should not miss this show. Thanking them again, I told them that the next show would be at two p.m.

During all this time Powell was out in front, boosting up for the next performance and by the time I got out there, he had quite a crowd gathered. Powell was one of the best spielers I had ever heard and knew how to hold the people. I told him I would go get a bite of dinner and that he better go inside and watch Buster while I was gone but that I would be back in about twenty minutes and then he could go get his dinner.

We did not have much time to talk about the first performance, but I will say we were so happy for we knew everyone had like the show, and we were sure we would make some money.

When I got back to the show, I told Powell to go get his dinner but he said he was too excited to eat anything but I talked him into getting a sandwich and a cold bottle of beer.

After our second performance, all that you could hear around the town square was, "Have you seen Buster?" We certainly had a big day and also the next day was almost as good as the first but the third day the crowd had sort of thinned out, but at that we had a fairly good crowd to see the show. We made a clean up, as one might say and there was no stock for sale in this show. I forgot to mention that Powell had put up most of the money on this adventure and he was to receive one third of the net profits.

We were told by several hundred people, that we had put on the best show for the money that some of them had seen at twice the price, and some of the people came back to see it the second time, thinking that perhaps the audience would go up and accept our offer to wrestle with Buster, but they were disappointed for no one offered.

The next day was spent in delivering the canvas and lumber back to the parties we had rented them from, so on the morning following, we could get an early start for home.

It took us two days to make the trip home, so we had plenty of time to talk things over and what our plans would be for our next show.

After arriving home it was not long until we received letters from different towns in regards to our show, so Powell and myself made plans to buy a show tent, also arranged to get another wagon and more stock. We made a special trip to Oklahoma City, placing our order for the show tent which was fifty feet by seventy feet and had them rush this order through as fast as they could.

Our next performance was to be held in Enid, Oklahoma, as we had made all arrangements to show there as soon as the tent arrived. We had to use two wagons to carry all of our equipment. The tent finally arrived and we had loaded our wagons and were about ready to start out. It was about noon and the day was very hot and as I was about ready to put Buster in his crate, my father advised me not to put him in it as it was too hot. He thought it would be better to let him get all the fresh air he could get and suggested that we time him outside in the wagon. So we managed to move the trunk and canvas back in the center of the wagon, I then took a heavy chain and placed it around the center of the wagon bed.

I thought that this would be fine as he could not get out and would still have freedom and could keep cool. But it was not a success for in a few minutes Buster turned around in the center of the wagon and by doing this, he twisted his large three inch collar around his neck so tight that it burst a blood artery in his throat. Buster was so strong and powerful that he just tore the wagon all to pieces. We just had to keep out of his way while this was going on for if he had ever hit one of us with his paws, there is no doubt that he would have killed us instantly.

After he gave up and had fallen down through the wagon bed, breaking the coupling pole, there he was hanging by his neck to this chain, choking to death. As luck would have it, I had just sharpened my knife the day before and I got my knife out in a hurry and give that collar one lick with my knife and it came right in two and Buster fell to the ground. He was bleeding very badly and of course I thought that he was dead.

We finally got the wagon from over him and then I could see that he was still breathing. Big tears came to my eyes for I was so sure that Buster was gone but my father told me to go to town on one of his horses as fast as I could and get a doctor. This I did and the doctor and I lost no time in getting back to the park where Buster was and I was surprised to see that he was still alive but it looked to me that he had lost three or four gallons of blood.

This doctor I brought out, seemed to be frightened of Buster but I told him that there was no need to be, as he was about dead. He stood back about seven or eight feet and asked me to open his mouth, so he could get a look at his throat. The Doctor stood back so far from Buster that I could not see how he was going to tell if there was anything wrong with his throat. He told me to get some tincture of iron and take a hand full and put it right down his throat and that this would clot the blood so he would quite bleeding. I went back to town with the Doctor in his buggy as I left my horse in town when I went in after the doctor. I was not long in getting on his back and made fast tracks back to the park.

I managed to get quite a bit of this down Buster's throat and it was but a few seconds until the blood began to clot and he quit bleeding. I was so badly hurt that I could not keep from crying and also Powell was sniffling.

After having this big accident, the show was all over and maybe you think this didn't hurt, for we had made such plans and how much money we were going to make this summer and that we were going to buy our own wagons and horses, but all this turned into a dream.

Several days went by and Buster lay right where he had fallen from the wagon and the only thing we could do for him was to keep him cool, running water on him during the day. We built a shelter over him of limbs and hay so he would be in the shade as there was no chance of moving him for some time. He must have layed there in the same position for ten or fifteen days and he was beginning to get so thin. To tell the facts, I never had much hope of him ever getting well and no doubt, if he had been any other kind of animal, he would have died in a short time.

I was told by the Doctor to only feed him soft food, such as cooked sweet potato and also squash, give him plenty of fresh milk. So after laying there for about fifteen days without food, I cooked some sweet potation and added milk to it, this I fed him with a large spoon. I had to hold his head up so that he could swallow. He seemed to enjoy it, so from then on, I fed him plenty of this also soft boiled eggs and it was not long until Buster was able to feed himself but he did not look like the same bear. He had been in this one position for so long that a great quantity of his fur had come out and also faded to a different shade from the other side.

During all this time we had received letters from different towns inviting us to come with our bear and all that we could do was to write them about Buster's accident. Oh yes, I forgot to mention what we did with our tent as we still owed money on it, so we wrote the company and explained our misfortune and asked if it would be possible to take it back off our hands. We received a reply in a few days that they would take it back, so we only about thirty cents on the dollar. I knew that Buster would not be well for several months and that there was no use in keeping the tent.

You are probably anxious to know what happened to Buster. I knew that it would never do to put a collar back on him as it might break the artery again. I never once thought that he would be able to get up and go away for I thought that he was too weak. But one day I happened to be in the skating pavillion cleaning up and as I glanced toward the lake, I saw Buster wading out into the lake. He was no doubt anxious to get in the water to cool off but I knew he was so weak that he might get drowned. I ran over just as fast as I could and waded out into the lake about twenty five feet and the water was about three feet deep and just as I thought, Buster was so weak, he could not hold him head up above the water. I finally go hold of his head and kept it above the water so he could get his breath and screamed as loud as I could to my father to come and help me. He came running to the waters edge and I told him that I turned loose of Buster's head he would drown. I told him to get one of the teams and a long heavy rope and I would tie it around his waist and in this way we could drag him out of the lake. It seemed to me as though it took my father two hours to get the team harnessed and down to the lake.

By the time he finally did get there, there were a couple of young men who had come out to the park to bathe, who helped me. They brought the rope out to me and I put it around Buster's waist and we dragged him out to where the water was about a foot deep. At this place we unhooked the team and drove a large stake down and tied Buster to it so that he could not get any further out in the water.

The next thing was to figure out how we were to get Buster back to the shade or his crate. He always seemed to be much happier if he was near his crate. I managed to get a large dirt scraper and we dragged this out into the lake and put it in back of Buster. I then took the rope from his waist and tied it to the scraper, hooking the team onto the scraper, we hauled him out and took him under the shade tree which was close to the barn. I took a strap and put it around his hind leg and fastened him to the tree so he could not get away again.

It was not too long until Buster was able to stand up on his hind feet and also take his runs back and forth as he used to do but he was not the same Buster. I do not believe that he weighed over eight hundred or nine hundred pounds after going through all of this.

One morning I went out to feed him but found him gone. He had broken the buckle of the strap with either his teeth or front claws. The first place I went to look for him was to the lake, so I made a trip all around the lake looking for tracks in the soft dirt but found none. I knew of course that he was not drowned as I would have found tracks and this made me feel better.

I hurried back to the house and told my father just what had happened and father thought the best thing for me to do was, get on one of the horses and go to all of the neighbors and notify them that Buster was gone and for them to watch for him. Everyone surely did help me, for as soon as I would notify them of Buster's disappearance, they would start looking over their farms.

In a day or so one of the neighbors came over and said that they were sure that Buster was under their house. I asked them if they had seen him under there but they said no, but they could hear him. I beat it right over there as fast as I could, figuring that perhaps Buster had gone under their house but he had never done anything like it before and I was very doubtful that it was Buster. Well what do you think I found under the house when

I arrived? One of their old sows with a new litter of baby pigs. When I came out from under the house and told the farmer about it, he could hardly believe it. Well this was just another false alarm.

I was a little scared that someone might shoot Buster if they should find him on their farm doing some damage or perhaps they might think he would hurt them.

Everyone in town was on the watch for him as I had spread the news and of course most of them knew him and I knew they would notify me as soon as they had a trace of him.

Four or five days passed by and no sign or word of Buster and I had ridden all over the country, also had several boy friends, who had horses, to ride around and ask if anyone had seen him. We did not have even the slightest trace of him so I then figured that he must have rambled down toward the Wichita Mountains.

One morning I was on the far side of the lake and there I discovered his tracks, which were fresh, evidently he came there for a drink. Now maybe you think I was not happy, well right there and then I tracked him into a corn field which had about twenty acres in it and joined on to the park. He had worked his way well into the center of this field, making a bed out of the corn stalks. He evidently wanted to get away from everyone and be quiet. I thought this was an ideal spot for him so I left him right there for several weeks but tied him by his hind leg. He seemed to gain faster right there than any other place. Of course I took food to him and also water. I would lead him to the lake once in a while but never let him get into the water.

It was now getting towards fall so I took Buster into town to his large cage and cave. He seemed glad to get back there again. I tried to put him through some of his tricks but he did not like to do them, some of them he would refuse to do. He was eating very heartily and picking up in weight and once again was looking fine.

I had received a letter from my mother in California and she had asked me to come to spend the winter with her. Well I could not take Buster with me and both mother and father had asked me to dispose of Buster as they were afraid that some day he would injure me. I was now considering selling him and yet I hated to another thing was finding a buyer for a large bear like Buster.

There was a man who owned one of the largest saloons in town who heard that I was talking about selling Buster, so one day he asked me about it. I then told him that I was considering it, providing I could find someone who would be kind to him. This man said that he thought it would be a good advertisement if he built a nice cage in the center of the saloon and put Buster in it. We talked it all over and so I decided to let him have Buster but said that it would be several days before he could get the cage built and that I could not leave until after I had taken Buster over to the saloon and place him in his new cage. It must have been a week or more before it was finished and must say it was a very attractive cage and cost considerable to build.

The next thing was to find some one who could take care of Buster and this cage as it had to be cleaned every day or so and fresh sawdust placed in it. Buster would also have to get acquainted as it would be dangerous for a stranger to go in and out of the cage.

They finally found a young man who said he would not be afraid, so in a few days he had gone in and out of the café ten or fifteen times and Buster seemed perfectly satisfied to have him. I told him to feed Buster some candy once in a while and that I was sure both he and Buster would be attached to each other in a short time. I went in to see how they were getting along several times a day, also going into the cage and playing with Buster.

One day the young man went into the cage and forgot to lock the door behind him and Buster went out and right on through the saloon and into the alley and the caretaker tried to stop him but nothing doing, Buster kept right on going up the alley and toward the residential district. He would occasionally stop and turn over a garbage pail and eat what food struck his fancy. The caretaker followed him and whenever he would get within a few feet of him he would start out on a run so the caretaker decided that it was best for him to locate me.

News travels fast and in about an hour after Buster's escape, I found out about it and I wanted to come and take him back to the cage. I went directly to the saloon and found out just where he had gone, so the caretaker and myself started out. After we were about eight or ten blocks from the main part of time, we began to ask the residents as to whether they had seen anything of Buster. Of course by doing this, the news spread faster than ever a one person would call their friends on the phone and tell them about it and of course the story was exaggerated a great deal as it was repeated.

As we came from one residence, we noticed that up the street a short distance there were three or four women and their children running across the street and we hurried up there as fast as we could asking what was the trouble and one said that she had just received a phone call from a friend that the largest grizzly bear had escaped and already killed a child and was now in that district. About this time there came a couple boys running as fast as they could, telling us that the bear was in the next block in a backyard and that the bear had killed a dog. We rushed right over there taking the boys with us so they could show us just where Buster was doing his killing. We found the right backyard and what do you think I found, Buster had surely discovered something that he was very much interested in, a hive of bees. The bees were so thick that I was afraid to go in to get him, so I knocked on the back door of this residence, but seemed to have a hard time in getting an answer to my knock. Finally a lady came to the door but she was so excited she could scarcely talk. I told her there was no need to get upset about Buster as he had hurt no one and all he had done was to wreck their bee hive and that I would see that the damage was paid.

During all this time Buster was getting a grand feed of honey. I asked the lady if she had a piece of mosquito netting, which I could put over my head to keep the bees from stinging me and she said she did not happen to have any on hand but she could give me a towel in which I could cut two holes, so I could see what I was doing. After placing this around my head, she cut out the holes in it and I was ready to go after Buster. I had taken a rope with me as I knew that Buster only had a collar on and did not know if he would let me come up to him as he seemed to be having such a wonderful time on his rampage but he made no attempt to leave the hive so I went right up and tied the rope to his collar but the bees were so thick that I got stung several times on my hands. Buster must have been stung too but he did not seem to mind it as he was having too much fun.

After taking Buster through the yard and out into the street, I gave the rope to the caretaker while I went back to tell the lady that I would be back to see that the damage to the bee hive was taken care of and she said that it was alright, she was glad that no one was hurt and that I had captured the bear.

As we started down the street, taking Buster back, we met the Sheriff and the Marshal also two other men. They were all in a surrey and had high powered rifles with them. The Sheriff jumped out and asked if anyone had been hurt. I told him I was sure no one had been hurt but many badly scared and I also told him of how Buster had gotten into the bee hive and that as far as I knew, that was all the real damage he had done and I was sure that Mr. Hill would take care of that damage. I then suggested that the Sheriff drive up to the house where Buster had done the damage and talk to the lady.

They were all laughing at Buster, for he was a sight, he had honey all over his ears, head and paws. I took him back to his cage but before we could put him in it, he had to have a bath for he had bees and honey all mixed in his fur.

Mr. Hill was glad to see un bringing him back and was more than glad to hear that he had done no real damage for he had heard so many stories, he said he was sure he would be broke, paying all the damage suits.

Well you would be surprised to see how much business the saloon done that afternoon. Mr. Hill had to add two extra bartenders to take care of the customers and Buster was the main attraction, of course.

Mr. Hill was very anxious to have me take the job as caretaker of Buster but I explained that I was soon leaving for California to visit my mother and that I was sorry I could not accept for I thought so much of Buster and of course if I had not been leaving town, I would never have sold him. He then asked me what he owed me for my trouble of getting Buster back and I said whatever you think is right. He handed me ten dollars, for which I was very thankful and asked me if I would stick around for a little while and answer questions which were being asked and I'll say there were plenty put to me about all the things Buster had done the two or three hours he was loose.

One man asked me if Mr. Hill intended paying for the cow Buster had killed and had also eaten part of it. I asked him who the cow belonged to and he gave me the party's name. I then took him to Mr. Hill's office and had him explain the story to Mr. Hill and as they were well acquainted, he thought perhaps there was something to the story. Mr. Hill advised me to go to this party and find out just what had happened.

I arranged for a horse and buggy and drove out to see the farmer whose cow was supposed to have been killed. It was true that the farmer had a cow but she had not been hurt. It seemed that she had broken out of the corral, perhaps she might have gotten a scent of Buster but he was quite some distance form this place when we captured him. All the damage done there was the breaking down of the fence and no one was sure that Buster was the cause but of course they tried to attribute it to that.

When I reported to Mr. Hill just what had happened out there, he said he had received several reports and would I just go check on them but he had his doubts as to any truth in them. By midnight all the excitement of the loose grizzly bear, had quieted down, but Mr. Hill had had a good business so I guess it pays to advertise.

A couple of days later, there was a traveling Theater Troupe came to town and two or three of the actors came into the saloon and one especially tried to get familiar with Buster by reaching his hand through the bars of the cage and pulling Buster's fur. He said he used to have a pet bear but not as large as this one. The caretaker had just told him not to tease Buster as he might hurt him but the actor paid no attention to what he was saying. He had not teased him long until Buster turned real quick and bit a couple of his fingers so badly that they had to amputate them.

Well here was more trouble for Mr. Hill and when I heard the bad news, I went at once to see him and have a talk with him. I told him that I had never known Buster to hurt anyone. Mr. Hill said he had at least ten witnesses who saw this man teasing Buster by pulling his fur and also they had heard the caretaker tell him to keep his hands out of the cage and not to tease him. There were also four signs on the cage which read, "This is a Silver Tip Grizzly and is dangerous, Please do not tease." But nevertheless this actor in a few days brought suit against Mr. Hill for Ten Thousand Dollars damage. By this time Mr. Hill was very much worried and did not know if it would be best for him to keep Buster for if he was going to cause him so much trouble, it would be better to dispose of him.

I went to see the actor who had lost his fingers, and find out if there was some way in which he would compromise with Mr. Hill. He said what he should do way, to get a gun and go right over and kill that bear. This surely hurt my feelings, so I told him the bear originally belonged to me and that Buster was very kind and had never hurt anyone during all the time I had owned him, and I did not think it was right to bring suit against Mr. Hill for that amount of money. I also told him that if he had heeded the signs and not teased Buster, he never would have been hurt. He then denied ever putting his hand in the cage. I then asked him if he did not put his hand in the cage, how did Buster bite you? I knew that Buster could not get any part of his head through these bars and only about an inch and half of his nose and that it would be out of the question for Buster to bite him unless he had his hand in the cage. I asked him to come over with me and I would show him that it would be impossible for Buster to bite him on the outside of the cage. It was even difficult for Buster to get his paws through the bars.

The actor said that the bars were bent at least two or three inches at the place where Buster stuck his head through and bit him. I told him that I had seen the cage shortly after the accident and that I examined it very carefully and that there was no place where the bars were bent over a half inch. He finally got very angry with me, stating that Mr. Hill had sent me over to talk with him, trying to get him to drop the case.

I told him that Mr. Hill was a might fine man and that if he would go to him and talk it over, I was sure that Mr. Hill would pay his doctor bill and no doubt give him a few hundred dollars besides. The actor then asked "Would you be willing to lose two of your fingers for Ten Thousand Dollars." I told him, of course no one likes to lose any part of their body but that he had caused it himself. I also told him that the caretaker had told me that he had once owned a pet bear but no doubt that it was a cinnamon bear and of course they are not dangerous as a grizzly bear and that he should have realized that Buster was a stranger to him and that he should keep his hands away from Buster.

Nevertheless I had no luck in getting him to drop his suit or have it settled out of court. So it came up for trial and as Mr. Hill had so many witnesses against the actor, the court did not even allow the actor his attorney fees or for his doctor bills. It was too bad for I know that Mr. Hill felt very sorry for him and that he would have been willing to have paid his doctor bill and given him some money besides, but the actor did not want to compromise or even talk to Mr. Hill, so the court made the decision.

Now as I had made all plans to leave Hobart for California the next week, I thought that I would go in and have one more talk with Mr. Hill regarding Buster and when I got hter he said, "Why you are just the person I wanted to see for there is a road show in town called "The Roosevelt Show" and travels in wagons. One of the owners came into the saloon and saw Buster and he was very much taken with him and came in to see me, asking me if I would sell the bear. He also wanted to know if Buster could do any tricks and I told him that he was very well trained and that the young man from whom I bought the bear, was still in town and that I would get him to come down and put him through some of his tricks. So what do you think of it? I think it is best for me to get rid of Buster as long as you are leaving town and this is a good chance, don't you think so."

Of course I hated to see Buster sold as I knew it would probably be the last time I would ever see him if he left Hobart, but I could not blame Mr. Hill either. I told him I would see what I could do with Buster first as I had not put him through any tricks for several weeks. Mr. Hill said, "Well if you are successful in getting him to put on a good performance, and I sell him, I will give you twenty five dollars." I told him I would do my best.

You see ever since Buster had his accident, I had not put him through much of his training and he did not do the tricks as he used to do them and in fact some of them he refused to do but I did manage to get him to do some of them very well.

Mr. Hill then sent for the owner of the show to come over to see the bear put through his tricks. When he came over, Mr. Hill introduced us and I then explained to him all about Buster, from the time I captured him up to the present time. After spending about an hour of putting Buster through his stunts, I told him it had been several weeks since Buster had done any of these tricks and no doubt if they had a good trainer, they would have no trouble in getting his to do all of them and could probably teach him many more new ones.

The show owner decided right there and then to buy Buster and wanted me to go along with the show as his trainer. I told him it would be impossible as I was leaving for California and they made me all kinds of offers to try to induce me to accept the position. I would have liked to have gone with them but I knew that both my mother and father did not want me to do this, so I just let the opportunity slip by.

Buster's new owners were very proud of him saying that he was the finest bear they had ever seen and were sure that he would make a lot of money if they could just get him started right. I think they paid Mr. Hill two hundred fifty dollars for Buster of which I received twenty five as my commission which had been promised me.

I took Buster down to where they had their show but they had no place to put him but said they were going to take one of their animal cages in which they had some leopards, and put Buster in that. I looked it over and told them I was afraid that it was too light weight, for if Buster took a notion to get out of it, he would have no trouble in doing so.

At this time there was another man that came upon the scene and I was introduced to him, they told me he was to be Buster's new keeper and trainer. To my recollection this man was a foreigner, just what nationality I do not know. But I do know that he was a very large man, weighing two hundred pounds or more. He asked me to put Buster through some of his tricks so that he would get an idea just what he could do and how I went about it, making him do them.

I had Buster do quite a few of his tricks and the trainer thought he did them very well and said he was sure he would have no trouble with Buster. He also that he had several good tricks he was going to teach him and as he had been an animal trainer for years, I need not worry about Buster, that he would be kind to him, also that he was sure that he and Buster would be good friends.

Now the hardest part of all was that I had to tell Buster "Goodbye". I hugged him several times and tried my best to keep the tears back but it was impossible. I was sure that I would never see him again as there was no telling as to where this show would be in another year and I did not expect to be back in Hobart for another year. He licked my hand and seemed to know that there was something strange going on.

The show pulled out of town the next morning and I did not get to see Buster again. I left in a couple of days for California and had only been in California a week or so when I received a letter from a friend of mine stating that Buster had been killed. He said that the trainer was trying to put Buster through some of his tricks when all of a sudden, Buster grabbed hold of him with his front paws, squeezing him, breaking several of his ribs and shoulder blades. They had to shoot Buster to make him let go of the trainer and did not know at that time if the trainer would live. They only had Buster three days and here he was shot. My, how this did hurt me when I received this news. My mother said, "That is just what I have always been afraid of and would happen to you, for you were so careless with Buster. You thought he would never hurt anyone, but you see what he did." Of course, I had to agree with her to a certain extent but I still feel that Buster would never have done that to me. I really think that the trainer tried to force him to do things he did not want to do. If he had only waited until he became better acquainted with Buster, he would probably had no trouble with him. Well it was the end of the most wonderful pet I ever had.

Several years later I made a trip back to Oklahoma and learned all the details of Buster's death also that the trainer did not die of which I was very glad.

After Buster was shot, he was shipped back to Hobart and sold to a butcher who then retailed the bear meat out at a dollar per pound. I had quite a long talk with the butcher and he told me that Buster dressed out at seven hundred fifty pounds and that he had no trouble in disposing of every bit of the meat. He then told me that he had the hide mounted and that it was certainly exquisite and said he would like to have me see it. I asked him if he would sell it and he said, "I should say not, that is one thing I would not sell at any price."

A few days later I went with him to his house to see the mounted hide and what a beautiful thing it was, I just begged him to sell it to me, but no matter what I offered him, he refused to sell. Thus ends the story of my pet "Buster the Grizzly Bear."

T.F. Briles, Hobart Oklahoma

Mary Jane Briles on a hunting and camping trip circa 1915

Twin Rocks Hotel, 1918, replica of the Dyerville Hotel

nklin . Briles
.8 N. Westmoreland Ave.
os Angeles, Calif.

BUSTER THE SILVER TIP GRIZZLY.

By Franklin T. Briles.

Before I start to tell my story of my Pet, which was a trained silver tip grizzly bear, I want to give you an idea as to the different species of bears. Science has found that there are over twenty species, there being five different kinds of grizzlys, some of which especially in California, have become extinct in the past twenty-five years. These grizzlys vary in size, some attaining the we of over a thousand pounds. The color varying from a buff shade a very dark brown, but when coming out in the spring after hiber nating, the hairs are tipped with silver, thus giving them the name of silver tip grizzly.

From the earliest history in America, the grizzly has been known as the fiercest and most dangerous of big game. To the Indian, it was considered a very high honor to obtain a necklace og grizzly claws. But the whiteman with his high powered guns have changed conditions so that the grizzly is much more shy than before, for at the slightest noise he will run away at a surprisingly rapid speed. The grizzly is very dangerous and if cornered will put up a fight and many hunters have been killed by them, especially if the bear is wounded. The grizzly is considered the most intelligent of all of the species andnto my knowledge is more intelligent than any other animal. Their sense of hearing is very keen and their scent is as good as a deer, being able to scent their enemy at a great distance. Their eyes are very small but have the keenest of sight. They have forty-two teeth, the same as the dog and are car- niverous, eating besides animal flesh, fish, birds s, leaves, ruit even

First page of the typewritten manuscript from 1926

Franklin T., sons Franklin S, Paul and Mayme at the Seven Oaks Resort in the San Bernardino Mountains. circa 1931

About the Author

Born in 1886 in Hobart, Oklahoma, he was well known as an entrepreneur, story teller and quite a character. Franklin's mother, Mary Jane Briles, left Oklahoma without her family, a family mystery to this day. She traveled via the Oregon Trail to Dyerville, California. She operated a hotel and stage depot for A.P. Cross, her son in law. The line ran between Eureka and Willitts. T.F. Briles, Franklin's father, owned and operated a feed store and mill in Hobart as well as the lake pavilion where Buster performed. Franklin divided his adolescence between his mother's home in Dyerville and his father's place in Hobart. He eventually settled in the Los Angeles area and married the girl next door Anna May "Mayme" Stevens. He was employed in the farm equipment business and was a very successful salesman. He was promoted to district manager which was the foundation for designing and building a state of the art tractor named the BritraCk. Investors were secured and manufacturing started.

He built a custom home, currently listed with the Los Angeles Historical Society and lived there for 6 prosperous years. One of the modern features of the home at 251 Borendo Street was the outside delivery door for the iceman. Every summer the family would drive their Buick and later their Packard at 30 mph to San Onofre Beach. They camped for 7 weeks at the Hula Hut for $1, used also for the set of a Marion Davies movie.

In 1929, The Great Depression left Franklin and his family with nothing but the pioneering spirit.

They did as most Americans did: they made do. 1930-32 the family spent some recovery time running a hotel in the redwoods near Laytonville before returning to Los Angeles.

In order to provide food for themselves and others, the family continued to hunt and fish at their Alder Grove Camp in Klamath, California. To make ends meet, they canned and sold salmon. During the winter the family was back in Los Angeles making Franklin's patented trailer hitches, dart boards and ouiji boards. They also spent many a working vacation in the San Bernardino mountains fishing, hunting and taking people horseback riding.

Throughout his life Franklin never lost his passion for adventure, hunting, fishing and the love of family. Pictured with him are his sons Franklin S., Paul and wife Mayme at the Seven Oaks Cabin Resort in the San Bernardino Mountains. He passed away in 1941 at the age of 56.

EPILOGUE

Most of the mighty Grizzlies and their habitat are now a
part of history as is the story of Franklin and Buster.
Our family would like to donate a portion of the
proceeds from this book back to nature.
In this way, we hope to sprinkle some peace on Buster's tragic ending.

With Love,
Franklin Stevens Briles and Susan Briles Lyon, 2009

www.ingramcontent.com/pod-product-compliance
Lightning Source LLC
Chambersburg PA
CBHW031238280526
45784CB00004B/1627